My Cup of Tea

Musings of a Catholic Mom

By
Danielle Bean

Pauline
BOOKS & MEDIA
Boston

Library of Congress Cataloging-in-Publication Data

Bean, Danielle.
  My cup of tea : musings of a Catholic mom / by Danielle Bean.
     p. cm.
  ISBN 0-8198-4837-9
  1. Mothers—Religious life. 2. Catholic women—Humor. I. Title.
  BX2353.B43 2005
  248.8′431—dc22

                              2004014512

The Scripture quotations contained herein are from the *New Revised Standard Version Bible: Catholic Edition,* copyright © 1989, 1993, Division of Christian Education of the National Council of the Churches of Christ in the United States of America. Used by permission. All rights reserved.

Chapters 6, 11–13, 15–18, 21, 24, 25, and 29 first appeared in *National Catholic Register* in serial form. Chapter 2 first appeared in *Our Sunday Visitor;* chapter 7 in *Envoy,* chapter 20 in *Pregnancy;* and chapter 23 in *Christ Our Light.*

Cover photo: Mary Emmanuel Alves, FSP

Interior photos: Mary Emmanuel Alves, FSP; excepting pages 28, 67 by Gordon Alves.

"P" and PAULINE are registered trademarks of the Daughters of St. Paul

Published by Pauline Books & Media, 50 Saint Pauls Avenue, Boston, MA 02130-3491.

Printed in U.S.A.

www.pauline.org

Pauline Books & Media is the publishing house of the Daughters of St. Paul, an international congregation of women religious serving the Church with the communications media.

  2 3 4 5 6 7 8 9   11 10 09 08 07 06

To My Family:

For my cherished husband Dan—
my toughest critic,
my biggest supporter, and the love of my life.

For my children Kateri, Eamon, Ambrose,
Juliette, Stephen, and Gabrielle—
the six little people without whom
I would have plenty of time to write,
but nothing to say.

Contents

Introduction

In order to help you understand my approach to writing this book, I should begin by telling you a little bit about who I am and what I do.

I fill sippy cups. I break up spitting fights. I read *Curious George Flies A Kite* several times a day. I do not, however, read in-depth analyses of the daily news, nor do I research writings of the saints or doctors of the Church. I am just a mom seeking to know and do God's will on a daily basis and meeting with varying degrees of failure and success. In other words, I'm no different from many Catholic women.

Busy mothers' thoughts are subject to interruption at any hour of the day, and our attention spans are incurably short. For these reasons, we need bits of inspiration that we can grasp in a few spare moments. We need deep thoughts that will stick with us long after we put down the book to chase a naked toddler.

In this book I have tried to share small thoughts in a way that can be beneficial whether they're read all at once or browsed through in scraps and spurts through-out a busy mother's day. The chapters have been written over the course of a few years and arranged according to subject matter—you'll notice that my family has grown along the way.

I have to be honest, though. It's true that misery loves company and that is part of what compels me to share my less-than-glowing moments in the following pages. There are times when all an exhausted mother wants is an opportunity to unload her complaints on a sympathetic ear. We want to confess: "I am tired of sticky little hands pawing at my face; I can't find time to scrub the bathtub and I'm not sure I even want to; and if one more person asks me to cut the crusts off a sandwich or tie a wet shoelace, I am going to lose it!"

In trying moments, we want reassurance that our feelings are normal, shared by many women, and that we *will* survive them. In my own life, I find that the most beneficial glimpses of spiritual insight and encouragement come through personal conversations with like-minded women who share their life experiences, help me to find humor in my struggles, and keep me focused on my goals. That's the kind of sharing that I hope to accomplish in this book.

Of course, there is more to my motivation than sharing misery. My faith and my family bring me an abundance of joy. When I slow down enough to recognize it, I know that my heart spills over with the goodness of God's grace. When a simple soul is filled with such an overwhelming surplus of undeserved blessing, it's hard to keep the good fortune to oneself. Thus, the biggest part of what I hope to accomplish here is to share the bounty—with my friends, with my neighbors, and with you. As it turns out, happiness loves company, too.

1

My Cup of Tea

Embracing the Mixed Blessings of Parenthood
2001

The gentle beginnings of sunshine filter through my kitchen window. The air is just cool enough to make a sweater feel cozy. Chickadees chatter and play at the outdoor feeder. It is a beautiful morning, but what I relish most about this particular morning is that so far, I am alone in it. I just nursed the baby and he is now silent in his crib. My husband and other children are still dozing. Even the dog merely groans and shifts his sleeping position as I shuffle past. The refrigerator hums and the clock ticks. The kitchen tiles press clean and cold against my feet. What to do?

I almost panic. Every mother knows this moment—a rare, precious instance when we find ourselves unexpectedly alone and surrounded by quiet and opportunity. My eyes search the room. Unload the dishwasher? No, too mundane. Start a load of laundry? No way. Then my eyes land on the teakettle. Of course. I will have a quiet cup of tea, I decide. A quiet cup of tea all by myself. What luxury!

While the water heats, I select my tea cup carefully. I choose a ceramic mug featuring a red barn and a green mountainous landscape dotted with pasturing cows. "Vermont" is printed in the lower corner. This is my favorite mug. I bought it in a little gift shop just hours after my husband proposed to me on a picnic blanket in a pretty country field in Vermont. I have stubbornly held on to the mug through the years as a reminder of that special time in our lives—a time when we would drive to Vermont for the afternoon simply because it was a nice day for a picnic. Now, as parents of five young children, those days sometimes seem far away. This mug seems the perfect choice for my quiet cup of tea this morning.

I fill the mug and am on my way to the rocking chair when I hear something. It's a tiny squeak. It's a squeak that the baby's crib makes. It squeaks when he kicks. He kicks before he cries. I stand a few feet from the rocking chair, holding my mug and holding my breath. The squeaking gets louder. I glance at the clock. He can't be hungry; maybe he'll go back to sleep. A whimper emanates from the bedroom. He's not really crying, I tell myself. He'll probably go back to sleep. The whimper grows louder, then turns to a wail. I set my mug on the counter and race upstairs to pick him up before he wakes anyone else.

I return downstairs with my crying infant, a tiny intruder upon my solitude. I try to nurse him. I check his diaper. I wind up pacing the floor and bouncing him in my arms. This soothes him. At last, he lets out an enormous burp and promptly falls asleep in my arms. I carry him carefully back upstairs and gingerly place him in his crib. He stays asleep, so I slip back to the kitchen.

I think I still have some time before anyone else wakes up, so I return to my cup of tea. This time I make it to the rocking chair and sit down with my steaming mug. After one or two sips, I hear a different noise. This time it is the sound of toddler feet scampering across the wooden floor and chubby little hands working at the bedroom doorknob until it gives way. Within minutes, I am face to face with Juliette, my fuzzy-pajama clad two-year-old daughter. "Come up," she announces as she scrambles into my lap. "Want some," she declares as she lunges for my tea. I adeptly balance her on my knees and hold the mug away from my body and out of her reach until she settles in my lap and snuggles against my chest. This is not so bad, I think, sipping my tea. I am not exactly alone, but at least she is quiet and willing to just snuggle.

Then I feel something. It is a cold wetness seeping through my pants and onto my leg. My cuddly early-morning companion is soaked and leaking. I scoop her up and sneak upstairs to find her a change of clothes. I tiptoe to the dresser and stealthily open a drawer. I fumble a bit in the dark and jump at the sound of my six-year-old daughter Kateri's voice, "Is it morning or what?"

"No," I try to convince her. "Go back to sleep."

She is not convinced. "Then why are you guys up? Do I have to stay in bed?"

Before I can think of a reasonable response, I am interrupted by the raspy voice of my three-year-old son Ambrose. "I need some juice." He squints at me expectantly in the dimly lit bedroom.

"Hey, how come no one got me up?" Now it is five-year-old Eamon. I sense defeat, so I surrender. I lift the bedroom shades, change diapers, dress the little ones, and head downstairs where I pour juice, make oatmeal, and unload the dishwasher.

I don't think of my tea again until later that morning when I am vacuuming the living room and I spot my mug, still full of tea, near the rocking chair where I left it. The pasturing cows seem to mock me. "You thought you could have a cup of tea this morning!" they laugh and moo. "You don't have time for tea. Tea is for other people!"

I resolve to reheat my tea as soon as I finish vacuuming, but I am immediately distracted by the sound of Kateri calling my name. She is in the front yard and apparently the dog has stolen one of her Beanie Babies. When I approach him to retrieve it, he lowers his head, growls, and takes off running. The children shriek with delight at the sight of their mother chasing an obviously more athletically inclined creature. Eventually, I do tackle him, and with a great deal of pleading and prying, I manage to extract a stuffed parrot from his jaws.

Hours later, I am fixing a row of peanut butter and jelly sandwiches in the kitchen when Ambrose brings me my cup of tea from the windowsill where I left it. The cows are smug. I give them a dirty look and place the mug on the counter. While the kids are eating lunch, I determine to defy those cows. I put my mug in the microwave to reheat. Behind me, I hear a thud followed by a gasp. I whirl around to see a gallon of milk on its side on the kitchen floor. As I watch, it glugs its contents into an ever-widening pool of white. Eamon stands guiltily beside it.

I know what they say about spilled milk, but I feel like crying anyway as I mop up the mess with a dish towel. The cows are right, I think bitterly. I can't even drink a cup of tea. With envy, I think of women whose lives aren't filled with constant distraction, women who have time for tea. I long for their organized, orderly, tranquil lives.

A few hours after lunch I am doing the dishes, still nursing my sour mood, when Eamon approaches. With a little smile, he hands me a piece of paper. It is a drawing of a blue koala bear surrounded by hearts. He heard me say once that I like koalas, and he knows that blue is my favorite color, he explains. He gives me a hug and walks away. There is no particular reason for this gift. He just loves me and wants to make me happy.

His gesture reminds me that although I may not have time for tea, my time is well spent.

Later that evening, I come across my cup of tea in the microwave when I am cleaning up after dinner. I pour the cold, dark liquid into the kitchen sink. The cows are quiet as I wash the mug, dry it, and return it to the cupboard.

Sometimes the endless tasks that fill my days seem insignificant, but I know the work I do is tremendously important to the five little people who are most important to me. My children occupy almost all of my time and energy. They constantly challenge me to be a better, more patient, more generous person, and they repay me with blue koala bears and unconditional love.

That, I realize with a triumphant smile, is my cup of tea.

2

My Hands Are Full
The Many Blessings of Many Children
2001

I am pregnant. I am sweating. My shoulder aches under the weight of an overstuffed diaper bag. I awkwardly shift my twenty-pound daughter from one hip to the other and pile a stack of Easy Readers, animal encyclopedias, and dump-truck books in front of the middle-aged librarian behind the desk. She glances at my two oldest children idling near the door and smiles stiffly at my two-year-old son who is affixed to my leg. She surveys all four children through wire-rimmed glasses as she methodically signs out each book we have chosen. "Well," she huffs as she slides the stack toward me and eyes my swollen belly. "You certainly have your hands full." Her tone is not encouraging, so I nod, smile, and usher my gang out the door.

We drive to the grocery store, and while waiting at the checkout, a man in line behind us counts my children and wonders aloud about their college funds. After checking to be sure that they are all mine, he shakes his head and runs a hand through his thinning hair. He purses his lips and tells me, "Better you than me, lady. You've got your hands full." I smile in agreement as I remove a candy bar from my two-year-old's hand and return it to the shelf. I accept my change and push my loaded cart to the parking lot.

At our next stop, the young bank teller is pretty and professional, with perfectly manicured fingernails and meticulously applied makeup. Her long hair is pinned up neatly and she is wearing a tailored business suit. She smiles and amuses the baby in my arms as she processes my deposit. When she notices the other children, however, she becomes sympathetic: "Ooooh, you poor thing," she coos to me. "I don't know how you do it. You have your hands full." She hands me my receipt and waves good-bye to the baby. I gather my children and lure them out the door with a promise of lollipops in the van.

We drive to the local playground and I let the older kids loose while I sit on a bench, keeping my littlest one nearby. I think about how often I have heard, "You have your hands full!" when I am out with my children. Some people are just making conversation, while others are expressing some form of disapproval or misunderstanding of our decision to raise a larger family. Perhaps one of these days I won't answer their comments with a nod and a shy smile. Perhaps instead I will point out that each of my children is an irreplaceable gift from God. I will inform the disapproving middle-aged librarian that I am honored that God has

entrusted my husband and me with the care of these dependent souls and humbled by the enormous responsibility that implies. I will tell the anxious man in the grocery store that it saddens me to realize how many people look at a group of small children and see only drudgery and financial burden instead of being awestruck by what tiny miracles they are. I will explain to the sympathetic bank teller that although my job may not be glamorous, being a mother is the most rewarding and satisfying work I have ever done.

Even if we have difficulty recalling our last unin-terrupted grown-up conversation, even if our budget doesn't leave much room for designer clothes or ele-gant cars, even if we collapse in exhaustion at the end of each day, my husband and I do not have less than most people; we have more. The unique joy that each of our children contributes to our family is immeasur-able. As our family grows, our hearts do too.

As I sit on the playground bench and reflect on the morning's events, my youngest daughter scales my leg and scrambles into my ever-shrinking lap. Within a few minutes her older brother also claims his place there. I balance the two of them on my legs and watch the older children climb the monkey bars. I press them both close to my heart as I think, "Yes my hands are full. Thank you, God, that my hands are so wonderfully full."

3

Time Flies

Gaining Perspective
2002

My two-year-old daughter is an exhibitionist. At every opportunity, she sheds her clothes, including her diaper, and leaves them in every corner of the house. This endearing habit leads to some messes (she isn't potty trained) and some embarrassment (we do occasionally have guests). We have tried bribing, punishing, distracting, scolding, and ignoring, but nothing seems to stop the stripping. So, what am I going to do?

I am going to wait.

Next month, my daughter will find some other means of trying my patience, or perhaps she will become a temporary angel and another of my children will take over the responsibilities of "family rascal." The one thing I am sure of, though, is that one day the strip show will stop.

I have not always had such perspective.

For example, my first child was a particularly difficult infant. From the moment she was born, her gaze penetrated mine in a most unnerving way. She was not at all the passive, defenseless creature I had spent nine months imagining. Her small body felt stiff and solid beneath the blankets. Her legs kicked hard against the swaddling. With her intense stare, she seemed already to be checking me out, this mother she had been born to, and evaluating my fitness for the job. My new daughter was strong, bold, and confident.

I wasn't.

In fact, she soon found out how hopelessly incompetent I was. During the weeks following her birth, I spent my nights pacing the hallway of our small apartment, jiggling her in one arm and patting her back. She spent those nights crying.

"Colic," pronounced the pediatrician, and he sent us home with a "How to Soothe Your Colicky Infant" pamphlet. My husband and I read it intently, looking for a magic cure. As the experts suggested, we tried warm baths, gas drops, infant massage, pacifiers, and running the vacuum cleaner. Nothing stopped the relentless crying.

I worried that my baby was in pain. I imagined that her tiny face turned purple with rage at my nervous awkwardness, hopeless ineptitude, and complete inadequacy. Mostly, I worried that I was a bad mother.

"Enjoy every minute," old ladies at the grocery store would warn me when they peeked at my sleeping bundle. "They grow up so fast." I always smiled in

agreement, but inside I was convinced they were wrong. This baby would never grow up. The weeks since her birth had been an interminable whirlwind. In fact, I remember one particularly trying night when I collapsed upon the bed, my back and shoulders aching, and sobbed to my husband, "I'll never sleep again!" I really believed it. I hadn't slept, showered, or eaten a balanced meal in what seemed like weeks, and in my delirious desperation, I was certain that things would always be so.

Several years and a few children later, I can now smile at the memory of those colicky nights and my early months as a mother. More so than any other life experience, motherhood has taught me that nothing does last forever. Just as the sweet moments of parenthood are fleeting, so too are the trials. It seems the old ladies were right after all.

I recently gave birth to my fifth child, a son who, moments after his birth, stared into my eyes with a look of familiar intensity. He cried inconsolably at the hospital. He still cries at home. He screams from my shoulder as I fold laundry and prepare dinner. He shrieks with rage as I cradle, rock, cuddle, sway, and pat him.

Together, we pace the cold wooden floors until at last, in the early morning hours, when his strength is depleted, he rests his small, sweaty head against my chest and draws deep, shaky breaths. I close my eyes and inhale the sweet scent of his soft, fuzzy head. This will not last forever. Babies do grow up.

Thankfully, with time, experience, and the grace of God, mommies do too.

4

Real Presence
The Importance of Friendship
2004

*B*ad nights lead to bad mornings. Last week the baby spent the better part of one night in my arms awake with a runny nose and a fever. She didn't want to sleep and she didn't want to nurse. She wanted to be wretchedly crabby in my arms. I stayed downstairs with my disagreeable companion until the early morning when I heard Dan's alarm clock ring upstairs.

He offered me a nod of sympathy and a pat on the shoulder before heading for the shower as the rest of our children came tumbling down the stairs wanting breakfast. Bleary-eyed, I set about changing diapers, brushing hair, and making oatmeal.

Soon after breakfast Dan warned the children to "take it easy" on their exhausted mother and left for work. I sat on the couch and held Gabrielle on my lap. She wiped her red, runny nose with the back of a hand and rubbed her eyes irritably. Dirty dishes filled the kitchen sink. A heap of wet towels and dirty pajamas covered the bathroom floor.

Juliette and Ambrose started an escalating argument over whose turn it was in a game of memory just as Eamon announced that a delivery truck was pulling into the driveway. I vaguely remembered Dan telling me that he expected a delivery of lumber that day. When the deliveryman knocked on the front door, I scrambled to find the checkbook and suddenly realized that I was still wearing my Tylenol-stained pajamas and had oatmeal in my hair.

Later that day, on the phone with a friend, I recounted my dreadful night and embarrassing encounter with the lumber deliveryman.

"Oh, that's nothing," she told me. "Once the UPS man caught me wearing nothing but a towel and threatening to spank my kids into next week!"

Her story made me feel better. Sometimes all we need in the midst of life's difficult moments is to know that we are not alone. Often I only want to share my personal grumblings with someone who can relate to the challenges I face as a mother of small children.

When my mom raised her nine children, there was an entire neighborhood of young families just outside her front door. The other moms on our block may not have always been the kind of people she usually befriended, but they had young motherhood in common—and that was enough. Today she still recalls being grateful for their presence, even if it was only to share occasional conversation.

When I look out the window of my home, though, I see ten acres of land and no neighbors. Because more mothers today work outside the home, even families who don't live in rural areas tend to be more isolated than families of a generation ago. Today's young parents, however, need community and companionship as much as ever.

Anyone with access to the internet knows the myriad ways in which virtual communities have risen up to meet this need. A quick internet search can open the door to thousands of potential cyber-friends who share our circumstances and are eager to empathize. I am always amazed by how easy it is to find friendly, helpful, faith-filled people online.

There is something to be said for the real presence of real friends in our own communities, though. Because Dan teaches at a small Catholic school, the families of the teachers there make up a community of young Catholic families. Their presence has been a true blessing to us. Among the wives of this group I have found friendship and support for my role as a Catholic wife and mother.

We bring meals to each other during family illnesses or after a baby is born. We gather for social events and arrange play dates for our children. The most valuable thing we offer one another, however, is our presence. I find great comfort just knowing that there are other women in my community who share my values and face the same trials I do on a daily basis. We are sisters in Christ, helping one another toward our heavenly goal.

After ending the phone call with my friend on that trying day last week, I sat in the rocking chair with my bad-tempered baby. She rested a sleepy head on my shoulder as the noisy antics of her older siblings revolved around us. Encouraged by a few moments of sympathetic adult interaction, I kissed the baby's head, instructed the kids to pick up their Legos, and planned what to make for dinner.

5

Growing Pains

Coping with Our Children's Pain
2002

Soon after my first child learned to walk, she experienced what every new parent dreads: her first real boo-boo. She was toddling about outside when she tumbled among some prickly vines. I quickly extracted her tiny, wriggling body, but she cried inconsolably for several minutes. The worst part was the long red scrape on her leg. Of course, it wasn't the kind of injury that sends you running to the doctor. Even I, a nervous new mother, knew that. It was, however, red and slightly swollen, a glaring flaw against her perfect porcelain skin. The look of it disturbed me. Clearly, I was not going to be good at this.

Eventually, as all mothers must, I became accustomed to the bumps and bruises of childhood. As the years went by, and I had more children, I mastered the fine art of kissing boo-boos better and brushing away small hurts. I learned the wisdom of pausing before rushing over to soothe a small injury. More often than not, I realized, my naturally resilient children recovered more quickly from a fall with no grown-up around to overreact. I always felt a certain sadness, though, when my little ones experienced their first real injuries. After months of soft flannel swaddles and loving caresses, a newly independent toddler quite suddenly is introduced to the harsh reality of bruised bottoms, bumped heads, and scraped knees. It's as if we are letting them in on a grown-up secret from which we've managed to protect them since birth. Welcome to the world, their new experiences seem to tell them. Life hurts.

I felt this kind of sadness most distinctly one recent day when I brought Ambrose, my four-year-old son, to the doctor. Ambrose has cystic fibrosis, or CF, an incurable, life-shortening, genetic disease that affects his lungs and digestive system. His medications and treatments keep him as healthy as possible, and, so far, his life is similar to most other children his age. Our greatest worries are for his future when the complications from his illness may become more serious. On this particular day, he and I were in the car, making our way through a driving downpour to his regular CF clinic visit, when he suddenly asked, "Why am I going to the doctor today? I'm not sick."

His earnest eyes met mine in the rearview mirror.

There is a part of every mother that seeks to shield her child from all forms of discomfort and disappointment, no matter how unrealistic that may be. That part of me ached now as I considered the best way to answer his question. Of course, my husband and I have spoken to Ambrose about his illness before, and he has always accepted that he needs some medication and care that other children do not need. This was the first time, however, that he seemed to notice that he was different and to wonder about that difference. This was the first time that he seemed to understand, on some level, that his body was not perfect. This was the first time that I gave him a name for his illness.

"Cystic fibrosis," he repeated cautiously, feeling the words with his tongue.

Up until this moment, Ambrose's illness had been a grown-up burden; it belonged strictly to those adults in his life who loved him and were responsible for his care. Now that he was old enough to understand some of its particulars, CF was becoming his burden too. I felt that I was letting him down. I loathed the emotional pain and disillusionment his illness might cause him more than I could dread any stomachache, infection, or physical discomfort he might ever suffer.

I tried not to say too much. I matter-of-factly gave him a few details about how CF affects his body and then resisted the urge to finish my explanation with something syrupy and cherubic like, "Don't worry. Everything will be okay." I held myself back from pretending it wasn't real or rushing in to soothe a hurt he could handle on his own. He shifted in his seat and

was quiet for a moment as he digested the things I had told him. I endured the aching silence and waited for his response.

"Well," he finally said, in the same casual tone he might use to tell me he doesn't want to go to bed or he would rather not eat his broccoli. "I wish I didn't have that."

He pressed his forehead against the edge of his car seat and stared out the window. Streaks of raindrops gathered and slid down the glass.

"Me too," I told him, and I parked the car.

We cannot protect our children from every pain, loss, or disappointment, and of course we shouldn't. To do so would be to deny them a vital part of the human experience. It wouldn't be reasonable to pretend that life is perfect, because it isn't. Sometimes it hurts. Sometimes it isn't fair. Sometimes we are disappointed. Our job as parents is to teach our children to handle the pains and frustrations they will undoubtedly face. They need to learn how to trust in the goodness of God, who gives us the strength we need and sustains us through the failures we experience in an imperfect world. When we allow our children to encounter life's inevitable pains and losses, we prepare them for greater challenges they may face in the future. In this way, our children become resilient, compassionate, and strong. In this way, we enable them to grow.

When we arrived home after the clinic appointment, the rain had cleared and wisps of white clouds streaked across a radiant blue sky. Ambrose scrambled from his car seat and rushed to join his brother and sisters, who were riding bicycles in the driveway. I watched him greet his siblings with a shout and drag out his own tricycle.

Just like everyone else, Ambrose's life will be a series of ups and downs, wins and losses, joys and sorrows. His experiences will not always be perfect, and as far as his four-year-old mind can comprehend it, he knows that now, more clearly than he did this morning. This is a loss for me, a painful letting go, but it is necessary step toward his becoming the grown-up I want him to be. I don't want to raise a son who shies away from difficulty and avoids discomfort at all costs. I want Ambrose to gain confidence and self-esteem by facing adversity and overcoming obstacles on his own. I want him to know that he needs God. These things cannot be accomplished painlessly.

As I watched, he balanced one foot on the pedal of his tricycle, paused, then swung his other leg over the bike suddenly and raced down the driveway. Rubber tires rumbled against the gravel. He approached a puddle, gathered speed, and then sailed right through, holding his legs out straight as water sprayed high from the back tires. He turned his laughing face upward, to the sun.

Suffering brings us closer to God. Pain and loss enable us truly to appreciate the sweetness of life's more joyful moments. These are truths Ambrose is beginning to learn, even as he teaches them to me.

6

Bear Instincts

With God All Things Are Possible
2003

I have always been a mouse. I don't haggle at yard sales. I apologize when other people bump into me. I cringe when my husband argues with a salesperson, even if he's right. I have always been a people-pleasing, bow-to-authority, don't-rock-the-boat kind of person, and for the most part, my meekness has served me well. I succeeded in school by striving always to please my teachers, and I thrived in the workplace by adeptly avoiding conflicts with my co-workers.

Things changed, however, when this mouse became a mother. Something about being responsible for innocent, defenseless, dependent human beings has made me less like a mouse and more like a Mama Bear. In fact, when it comes to protecting my little ones' safety and well-being, I can be assertive, aggressive, and downright confrontational. As a new mother several years ago, I was surprised to find myself suddenly approaching strangers with a nervy smile and saying things like, "Would you mind not smoking here? My baby's lungs are pink."

The mouse in me was aghast. She squealed with embarrassment the day I marched up to a rowdy group of teenagers at a public park and admonished them to stop using foul language in front of my children. On another occasion, I had to stop short to avoid hitting a car that cut me off in a parking lot. My mousy self covered her face with timid pink paws as the Mama Bear in me scolded the middle-aged man behind the wheel.

"Watch where you are going!" she reprimanded him. "There are babies in this car!"

It has been my experience that people tend to respect maternal instincts. The foul-mouthed teenagers may have rolled their eyes and snickered a bit, but they stopped cursing. The careless driver apologized profusely and left in a hurry. By nature, most people seem to know that it's unwise to aggravate a Mama Bear when she's protecting her cubs. Like cautious campers, they back off slowly, avoiding a direct confrontation.

One of my most memorable Mama Bear moments took place a couple of years ago when my then five-year-old daughter Kateri had to be hospitalized overnight due to dehydration from a stomach virus. My husband was away, so I left my two sons at my parents' house and took Kateri, along with my four-month-old daughter Juliette, whom I was breastfeeding, to the hospital. Kateri had an inordinate fear of doctors and needles, so I knew that going to the hospital would be difficult for her. To assuage her fears, I promised her that I would be with her every minute. I assured her that, no matter what, I would not leave her side.

When we arrived at the hospital, the baby slept quietly in her car seat while we filled out forms and checked into a room. When it came time for the IV, it took two nurses to hold down my hysterical daughter while a third inserted the needle. Juliette still slept.

When they were through, Kateri lay on the bed, exhausted and staring at the television set. I sat beside her and stroked her hair. A stout nurse strode into the room and hastily flipped through Kateri's chart. She scarcely looked at us, but I read her name tag: Margie. She checked the IV and was about to leave the room when Juliette awoke and let out a small gurgle. Startled, Margie looked in the direction of the car seat, then turned back to me.

"Will someone be coming to pick up the baby?" she asked.

"No," I explained, "she's breastfeeding, so I can't be away from her overnight."

Margie folded sturdy arms across her chest and peered down at me with forbidding eyes.

"You can't do that," she told me. "It's against hospital policy."

I explained that it would be impossible for me to leave the baby, and that I needed to stay with Kateri, but she remained unyielding.

"Only patients and parents can stay overnight. If you can't leave the baby, someone will have to replace you," she dictated. Then she breezed from the room.

And so I was left sitting on the bed, facing the impossible dilemma of choosing which of my children to abandon for the night. My stomach churned uneasily. I looked at Kateri. Her face was pale and thin. Her eyes were glazed. She might be okay if my mother stayed with her, I reasoned. I looked at Juliette, whose tiny feet kicked against the blanket as she cooed and played in her car seat. Maybe she would take a bottle, I considered.

Mama Bear, however, did not like this mousy line of thinking. After all, I had promised Kateri I would stay with her. It wouldn't be fair to go back on my word. Furthermore, Juliette had never taken a bottle. She might balk at the idea and go hungry for hours before I got back to her. It didn't seem right that "hospital policy" was requiring me to make such a choice. Mama Bear was righteously indignant.

Leaving my mousy self behind, I marched to the nurses' station where I found Margie, who was now seated behind the desk.

"What do you mean by 'hospital policy'?" I demanded. "Is it an official rule that my baby can't stay here, or is it just that you would prefer she didn't?"

Margie's eyebrows arched in surprise. She admitted that the rule was probably not an official one, but insisted that it was important to limit the number of people in the room for the sake of infection control.

I told her I wasn't concerned about my baby giving germs to her older sister. She was unmoved. I promised her that the baby would remain in her car seat or my arms at all times. She stared at me grimly. I argued that as someone interested in the welfare of children, she couldn't possible ask a mother to choose between her daughters. She only repeated that it was against the rules for my baby to stay overnight. Finally, I asked to speak to the head nurse, and she told me that she was the head nurse.

Prickly tension hung in the air between us. The conflict was more than my inner mouse could bear. I heard her squeaking to me from the room where I had left her. Give up, she was telling me. Say it's okay! Just leave!

Mama Bear remained resolute. I stood in front of the desk, clenching and unclenching my fists, enduring the hostile silence, and returning Margie's steadfast stare.

At last, she glanced sideways at some of the other nurses who had gathered around her desk and then turned back to me. Her eyes seemed to soften a bit. She sighed and waved her hand.

"Do whatever you think is best," she told me.

It was a relief to smile and thank her. The mouse in me was glad to see that she smiled back. I skipped back to my daughters and the rest of our stay was uneventful.

We can't predict the ways in which our children will change us. When we become parents, what was once good enough for ourselves, and even our spouses, suddenly isn't anymore. The responsibilities of parenthood quickly expose our weaknesses and challenge us to improve ourselves. More often than not, we are up for the challenge. Our parental instincts, a precious gift from God, empower us to become strong when we were weak, generous when we were selfish, and bold when we were timid.

My transformation from mouse to bear is a clear example of the way in which God provides us with grace and strength, skills and abilities according to our place in life. We need never doubt our ability to do God's will: "...For God all things are possible" (Mt 19:26).

I don't know if the Mama Bear in me will retire when my children are grown. I might return to my old ways of thanking police officers for traffic tickets and smiling at people who cut in line at the post office. In the meantime, however, put out that cigarette, watch your language, and for goodness sake, don't drive so fast.

I am Mama Bear. Hear me roar.

7

Shopping for Answers

Bearing Witness to Christ

2002

*I*n the grocery store parking lot, I boost my two-year-old daughter and my three-year-old son into a shopping cart and then heave the baby's car seat into the front. I remind my two oldest children to stay beside me and to walk around the puddles instead of through them, and together we make our way into the store.

Inside, I am at the deli counter, comparing hot dog prices, when I hear someone call my name. I turn around and recognize a woman I haven't seen for months. She is the mother of one of my daughter's swimming lesson classmates.

After saying hello, she counts the contents of my cart and exclaims, "Oh my goodness! You had another baby! Sweetheart, haven't you figured out what causes that yet?"

While I look at her, my mind racing to find an appropriate response, she adds, "Seriously, how many kids are you guys going to have?"

I open my mouth to answer, but find that I have nothing to say. I am struck dumb by the absurdity of discussing intimate details of my personal life with a near stranger while standing in the grocery store holding a package of hotdogs.

Thankfully, the sight of my three-year-old leaning out of the cart and maneuvering to dip his hand into the lobster tank distracts me. I excuse myself hurriedly and my inquisitor heads out the door.

I am never eloquent when I need to be. As I push my cart down the next aisle, I consider all the things I should have said to a woman who so clearly failed to understand why anyone would want to raise a larger family. I should have told her that each of my children is an irreplaceable gift from God. I wish I had described the special joy that openness to new life brings to our family. I wish I had said *something*.

This is a familiar frustration. It seems that words often fail me when it comes to defending my faith and the choices my family makes in the service of God. I must admit, too, that frequently I just want to fit in. I want to take my kids to the grocery store without becoming a public spectacle. I want others to greet new additions to my family with the same joy we feel instead of sympathy, confusion, or amusement. I want to be supported not challenged as my husband and I embrace God's will for our family.

Of course, I am longing for a world as it could be— a world where Gospel values are cherished and hon-

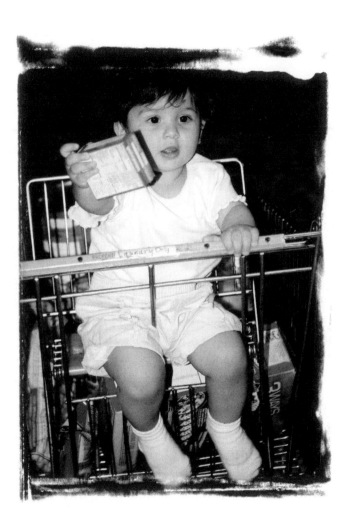

ored. Unfortunately, the "real world" is not that straightforward. Historically, God's faithful followers have never concerned themselves with meeting the world's expectations, only God's. Noah's neighbors chortled with laughter when he built the ark. An out-of-wedlock pregnancy was sure to cause problems, but Mary didn't reject God's will out of fear of her neighbors' judgments. Throughout the years, thousands of saints have lived, suffered, and died in the service of God, and only some of them managed to deliver eloquent sermons in answer to the worldly people who challenged them.

Sometimes words fail us. An old cliché tells us that actions speak louder than words, and I am grateful for the reminder. Even though I haven't been blessed with the gift of quick verbal answers to people's annoying and sometimes rude questions, my whole life is an answer.

Even if we dislike the attention it sometimes garners us, the way in which Dan and I choose to live out our commitment to marriage and children can be a powerful witness to those around us. If I push my boisterous shopping cart boldly past disapproving glances, if I remain unapologetic in the face of rude assumptions and ignorant questions, my family can be an example of Christian living in a secular world. My animated flock of children is a living, breathing, active testament to the wonder of God's love, the beauty of his creation, and the miracle of his goodness.

At the checkout, my children scramble to help unload the shopping cart. I say no to candy. I rescue the eggs from my two-year-old daughter while my five-year-old son struggles beneath the weight of a gallon of milk. I say no to candy again. The baby gurgles and drools, then flashes a toothless grin at the cashier. I say no to candy and don't ask me again. My three-year-old drops his stuffed tiger and his older sister crawls beneath the cart to retrieve it.

As we leave the store, three children ride in the cart, one hangs on the side, and the oldest helps me push. A man at the exit sees us coming and holds the door.

"Wow!" he exclaims as we pass by. "Are they all yours?"

"Yes," I answer brightly. "Isn't God good?"

8

A Dollar Between Us

Trusting in Divine Providence
2004

*L*ove is cheap. Years ago, when Dan and I were dating, he used to drive 100 miles from his college in New Hampshire to mine in Massachusetts to pick me up every weekend. We were young and in love—the miles didn't matter. Coming up with three quarters for the highway tolls, however, sometimes proved troublesome.

One Friday afternoon, Dan arrived at my dormitory to pick me up and confessed that he had no money for the return trip. I emptied my purse and came up with a couple of dimes and a nickel. Together, we then ransacked my dorm room reaching through dust bunnies under the bed and rummaging through desk drawers in search of spare change. We added up our findings: fifty-eight cents.

We were considering the implications of running through the toll booth without paying the full amount when suddenly I thought to check the pockets of a dirty pair of jeans in my laundry bag. There I found—

yes!—a whole dollar bill. I gasped and held it out for Dan to see. For a moment we stood speechless, holding the rumpled bill between us, astounded by our good fortune.

These days, we don't often have trouble paying highway tolls, but after ten years of marriage and six children, we still know the value of a dollar. We drive used cars, our dinner menus are usually determined by supermarket specials, and I never turn down an offered bag of second-hand clothing.

When Dan made the decision to teach at a Catholic boys' school, we knew that the financial rewards would be few. We have always trusted God to provide for our material needs, though, and he has never disappointed us.

I have found, however, that sometimes God tests our faith a bit before he provides. Once, when Ambrose's doctor prescribed a new medication that cost 1,500 dollars a month, our health insurance refused to pay for it. After spending the afternoon on the phone with the doctor's office, the pharmacy, and the insurance company, I found no solution. I called Dan at work and burst into tears.

"Don't worry," he reassured me. "If Ambrose needs that medicine, God will help us to get it."

After an anxious, heartsick weekend, I received a call from a nurse at the doctor's office. She explained that the pharmaceutical company had agreed to give us a six-month supply of the medication free of charge.

By the end of six months, our insurance coverage had changed and the prescription was covered.

Of course, we need to be prudent, and God expects us to use our natural gifts of intelligence and reason to make sensible decisions for our families. If we remember to put God first, though, we need never doubt his goodness and generosity. After all, our Lord teaches us: "Therefore do not worry, saying, 'What will we eat?' or 'What will we drink?' or 'What will we wear?' For it is the Gentiles who strive for all these things; and indeed your heavenly Father knows that you need all these things. But strive first for the kingdom of God and his righteousness, and all these things will be given to you as well" (Mt 6:31–33).

Recently our parish hosted a marriage preparation seminar for engaged couples. Being the nosy person that I am, I slipped into the conference room after Mass and glanced through some of the written materials they were using. In one booklet, under a section titled "Finances and Family Planning," one statement caught my eye.

"Children are expensive," it declared in bold print. The author then went on to highlight all of the costly material goods parents must buy for their children. He listed everything from diapers to strollers, and piano lessons to college tuition.

I wondered: Is this the message we want to reinforce? Our materialistic, contraceptive culture has already told young people to view children as expensive burdens a long time ago. Shouldn't the Catholic message concerning children and finances be an alternative, life-affirming one?

My faith and my experience tell me that children are a precious gift of marriage and God's choicest blessing. You can't put a price on the smooth fleshy arms of a baby, still warm from her nap, that reach around your neck and squeeze you as if you are the only person in the world who matters. You can't give a dollar value to the innocence and admiration of a child who watches his father play tennis and asks with earnest, "Is there anything Papa can't do?"

Children are expensive? There's no doubt that children must be fed, clothed, and educated, and that these things aren't free. When I consider the ways in which family life has changed us, though, I figure Dan and I are getting a bargain. Responsibility for children compels us to abandon selfishness and materialism. Through the joint venture of raising our family, making daily sacrifices and accommodations, Dan and I have grown in love for God and for each other.

Tonight at dinner, our children scuffle into their chairs and gather around plates of spaghetti, talking and laughing, exchanging jokes and stories. I look across the table at my husband and recall our humble college days with a dollar between us. Little did we know what wealth God had in store for us.

9

Every Mother Works

Blooming Where You're Planted
2004

The house was clean and the chicken cordon bleu was perfect. The children maintained reasonably good "company" behavior and then went uncomplainingly to their beds. Despite these successes, however, the evening we entertained two of my husband's old friends and their girlfriends several years ago, I felt like a miserable failure.

Throughout the evening the men shared high school reminiscences while the women talked at great length about their graduate studies in chemistry and biology. After describing her plans for a career in environmental biology, one of the women finally turned to me and asked, "So, what do you do?"

The room grew quiet. I suddenly felt very pregnant. In fact, my eight-month pregnant belly seemed to swell to twice its size as I managed to stammer, "Me? I- I'm just a mom."

There was a long, awkward pause while my new acquaintances considered what to do with this information.

"That's nice," one of them finally offered. "My sister has kids."

I can't remember what I said next, but I know it wasn't dazzlingly insightful.

"I used to be somebody!" I wailed to my unsuspecting husband as his friends' car pulled out of our driveway at the end of the evening.

Poor Dan. He said all the things a man is supposed to say when his wife is determined to feel sorry for herself, but I wasn't prepared to listen. I was acutely missing the simple sense of accomplishment and success of my younger years and I needed to stew for a while.

Most at-home mothers I know squirm in the face of the "What do you do" question. Although I know that the things I accomplish in raising my children are more valuable than any contributions I might make to society as a member of the work force, there are moments when I think longingly of my college years and yearn for a more tangible sense of success.

In my generation, a great deal of attention has been paid to the so-called "Mommy Wars" in which mothers at home are pitted against full-time career women. Most of the women I know who work outside the home, however, are not the glamorous, greedy, selfish career women some would have us envision. They are faith-filled women seeking to do what is best for their families, often at great personal cost to themselves.

After our first child was born, I worked full-time to support our family while Dan finished his coursework in a masters program. Although I enjoyed my work, and my mother took wonderful care of Kateri, my heart broke every time I had to leave her. I didn't work for personal fulfillment but out of financial necessity.

We can't always choose our circumstances. We are called to different states in life and we each have our own cross to bear. Some mothers sacrifice by staying home while others sacrifice by going to work. What we know is that if we willing and lovingly make sacrifices and work for the welfare of our families, God will bless us for it.

Christ tells us: "...Unless a grain of wheat falls into the earth and dies, it remains just a single grain; but if it dies, it bears much fruit. Those who love their life lose it, and those who hate their life in this world will keep it for eternal life" (Jn 12:24–25).

I am happy to report that in the years since that miserable dinner party, I have become more contented in my role as a full-time wife and mother. In fact, I thrive in the quietly supportive role God has given me and I am proud to be the indispensable, though often unseen, heart of our family life.

This afternoon, the kids come in from playing outside, pull off their boots, and wrestle out of their coats. Dan challenges Eamon to a game of chess and the younger boys settle in to watch as they set up the game pieces. The girls immerse themselves in an imaginary game of "Pretty Ponies."

Like my mother before me and my grandmother before her, like so many mothers all over the world, I stand at the kitchen stove while my family's life swirls around me. I add vegetables to the stew, squeeze the baby on my hip, and stand quietly stirring. Motherhood, in all its forms, is a steadfast, time-honored profession, and I am honored to be here.

10

Sweet Dreams

Serving God by Serving Our Children
2002

I awake to find myself cramped in the far corner of my bed, clinging to the mattress to avoid being pushed onto the floor. Rousing myself to consciousness, I find that my neck is stiff and my left side is asleep from the waist down. My husband dozes comfortably on his side of the bed, but my four-year-old son and my three-year-old daughter, along with their various sprawling limbs, have completely taken over my half of the bed. I have some blurry memory of "I had a bad dream," and, "Mama, pwease I sweep wif you?"

I get out of bed and squint at the alarm clock: 3:00 A.M. I rub my throbbing neck and shake my leg in an effort to restore its sensation. One at a time, I scoop the slumbering intruders from my bed and, despite an onslaught of protest, return them to their own beds. After one trip to the potty, two cups of water, several tuck-ins, kisses, hugs, and stuffed animal retrievals, I convince them to stay there. I think.

I stumble back to my own bed, smooth the mangled sheets, and crawl in. For a moment I indulge in the luxury of having one whole side of the bed to myself. I stretch my aching back and marvel at how far I can extend my legs without touching anyone else.

In the years since our first child, my husband and I have seldom spent a night alone. Much against our wishes, the little people in our lives have made themselves at home in our bed. We have tried bribing, threatening, scolding, and punishing, but so far each solution seems to work for only a little while. Slowly, our children come creeping back, little by little, until they have reclaimed what they believe to be their rightful place beside us in bed.

But isn't this just what children do? Without consideration for our own selfish inclinations, they work their way into our lives, demanding access to places that we had previously considered ours alone. One of God's greatest gifts to parents comes through our children's natural, dogged insistence that we abandon our own self-seeking in favor of theirs. Just as they push their way into beds, they bully their way into every aspect of our world, forcing us to accommodate them and, in the process, teaching our hearts to grow.

Children are born wanting, needing, and demanding. By nature, we are driven to meet their needs. In

this way, we are often surprised to find that our own wants and needs are not as important as we once believed them to be. Some might call this an instinctual drive, but I call it a gift from God. How many other people have so many tangible, obvious occasions to practice self-sacrifice in the course of their daily living?

Christ teaches us to see him in others, and our children are a natural place to begin. "How much do you love me?" He challenges us through their tiny voices. Will you take off all the snow gear you put on me minutes ago so that I can go to the bathroom and then put it all back on? Will you let me use your bridal veil to play princess? Will you buy the inexpensive, stain-resistant shirt instead of the one you really want? Though we may not always respond with perfect patience and generosity, the unpredictable and demanding nature of family life holds the promise of future opportunities to answer God's call to charity. If we recognize our weaknesses and learn from our failings, we can grow in our obedience to God and our love for others.

At the precise moment when I am falling back asleep, I hear a familiar sound. The shuffle of fuzzy pajama-clad feet is followed by a clumsy opening of my bedroom door. With a sudden flood of light, my three-year-old daughter enters the room. She marches boldly to my bedside and, without saying a word, clambers in, claiming her spot beside me. She snuggles her back against me, adjusts my pillow, and tugs at the covers until she is satisfied. I am too tired to resist. I drape my arm around her and pull her close. She heaves a heavy, contented sigh and rests a small hand on mine, patting gently.

11

Finding Our Wings

A Tangible Easter Message

2004

You can count on Wal-Mart. Every year, beginning the day after Valentine's Day, the retail giant's aisles overflow with rabbit-ear headbands, plastic peeping chicks, and talking, singing, dancing stuffed rabbits in your choice of springtime pastels. Chocolate bunnies peep out from wicker baskets and plastic hens sit smugly atop foil-wrapped candy eggs filled with caramel, marshmallow, and coconut cream.

"After Lent! After Lent!" I always say to my cartful of captivated children as we breeze past Easter store displays. While I am sure that merchandisers' pre-emptive Easter celebrations are financially motivated, I must acknowledge that the real message of Easter knows no season. In fact, one of my own favorite Easter moments took place a couple of years ago...in July.

My husband Dan was working late. Electric fans blew hot, humid air in all directions. The heavy odor of an overflowing kitchen garbage can hung in the air and sweat trickled down the back of my maternity blouse as I prepared dinner for the children. Gasping for breath, I plunked a plate of grilled hotdogs and chopped vegetables on the dining room table.

"Hotdogs?" one of the children moaned. "Didn't we have hotdogs already this week?"

"I'm not sure," I replied coldly, though I knew full well that hotdogs had been on the dinner menu a minimum of three times a week lately.

"Do we hafta' drink milk?" another child griped. "It's too hot to drink milk."

In brooding silence, I poured milk into four plastic cups.

Then as two-year-old Juliette reached across the table for her cup, she knocked over the other three. White liquid spread across the dining room table, dripped into the space between its leaves, and trickled onto the floor.

Anyone who has been eight and a half months pregnant or endured a stifling New England summer night without air conditioning will find it in their heart to forgive me for the way in which I was planning to respond.

Thankfully, though, we were distracted by a sudden thump and a scuffling just outside the front door. We hurried outside and were startled to find a small black and white bird, a chickadee, lying lifeless on the walkway.

Instinctively, I stooped to pick it up. The children gathered around and stared with hushed amazement at the tiny creature in my hands.

"Oooooh..." Juliette's eyes grew wide and her little lips formed a perfect circle.

"It must have flown into a window and died," I told her.

The bird was warm and almost weightless in my hands. Its eyes were closed and its miniature legs hung limply from my fingers. I extended one of its wings and examined its flawless feathers. Then I glanced toward the nearby woods and contemplated an appropriate burial ground.

Suddenly the children gasped.

"Look at its eyes!" they cried. "They're moving!"

The bird's eyelids fluttered and its wings flapped. We stood in quiet wonder as the tiny creature struggled, strained, and finally righted itself. Then the resurrected bird stood blinking in my cupped palms, turning its head from side to side. With a final fluttering flourish, it took to the air. We watched in silence as it arced gracefully into the sky, farther and farther away. It became a small speck on the horizon and then vanished from our view.

I like to think that we are like that little bird, helpless and weak in the hands of a loving God. We are bruised and broken by our sins. At the end of a long Lent, in the midst of sacrifice and daily drudgery, the

Easter message of hope, joy, and new life is beautiful and real, unexpected and astonishing. Our risen Lord transcends human suffering, and through him we are renewed.

At Easter we are resurrected. A triumphant Christ enters through our locked doors. He wipes away the tears of the sorrowful, invites skeptics to examine his wounds, and breathes upon the trembling to give them strength. Our Lord cradles us in his healing hands, gives us wings, and urges us to fly.

12

Resurrection Triumph

Gratitude for the Sacraments

2003

When my daughter Kateri made her first confession last year, I was a typical, hovering mother. "You've got your list, right?" I pestered her as she stood waiting outside the confessional. "If you forget what to say, just ask Father... Wait till he tells you to say your Act of Contrition... Listen to the penance he gives you..."

To her credit, Kateri didn't roll her eyes or shoo me away. She smiled nervously and nodded at all my last-minute instructions. Finally, when it was her turn, she stepped into the confessional and closed the door, leaving her anxious mother behind. Though I had never consciously planned to follow her inside, I was startled nonetheless to find myself quite decidedly on the outside of the heavy wooden door as it closed behind her.

There I stood, alone in the quiet, dimly lit church with nothing more to do than wait. I had done my part by helping Kateri learn her catechism and prayers, but now my presence was inappropriate. To a protective parent, this is no small revelation. Inside the confessional, my daughter was alone with God and what was going on between them was quite frankly none of my business.

Afterward, as she and I knelt together in the church, I thanked our Lord for his forgiveness as I always do after confession, but this time was different. I was thanking him not for the mercy he had shown me, but for the gift of forgiveness he had given to my daughter. As I gazed upon the crucifix, I understood clearly, maybe for the first time, that Christ had suffered the pains of the crucifixion for the sake of my child. Although intellectually I had always known that God loves my children more perfectly than I do, I had never really appreciated it in this way before. My daughter's sins were forgiven through the sacrament of Penance, not because I loved her so well, but because God did. It had nothing to do with me.

When it comes to material gifts, I appreciate the things people give to my children far more than I appreciate gifts for myself. As parents, we are always touched by the love others show for our children. Because we love them so much, when another person recognizes their worth and shows kindness to them, their actions are precious to us.

Now that Kateri was old enough to receive the sacraments, God was preparing to shower her with gifts far more valuable than any she had ever received

before. This made me recognize all the more clearly that my children belong to God. We may think we love our children limitlessly, but ultimately we are only earthly parents. All children are God's children first. He knows them best, gives them what they need most, and loves them even more than we do.

During this first Lent since Kateri's first confession, I am particularly grateful that it is not only for the love of me that Christ suffered, but for the love of all his children, including the ones he has lent to me. He endured the scourging at the pillar to gain forgiveness of sins my children have yet to commit. He suffered the crown of thorns so that my little ones might see heaven. Even as the nails were driven into his hands and feet, he saw my children's faces and loved them. He accepted death on the cross so that they might enjoy new life.

At Mass on Easter Sunday, as our children fill our arms and spill into the pew around us, I will thank the Lord for the blessing of our family. As we celebrate the miracles of his triumph over death and his victory over sin, I will appreciate these gifts more fully than before. Most importantly, however, I will thank God for loving my children so well. Through his passion, death, and resurrection, our Lord grants them mercy, forgiveness, and the promise of heaven; these are precious gifts even an anxious, over-attentive mother could never give them.

13

God's Tiny Messenger

Remembering What Matters Most

2003

I am preparing dinner. This means, of course, that eighteen-month-old Stephen is firmly affixed to my leg, piercing my ears with the high-pitched whine of an emergency vehicle siren. In a moment of inspiration, I abandon the browning hamburger, gather up my screeching ambulance, and plop him in his high chair with a bowlful of orange wedges. I have bought myself some peace, but it doesn't last long. Next, three-year-old Juliette and four-year-old Ambrose come tearing down the stairs each trying to out-shout the other in an effort to give me their own version of an argument first. "He won't share!" I make out, and, "She's ruining everything!"

Still feeling inspired, I decide to distract them with some music, a recently purchased, still-exciting "Veggie Tales" CD to be exact. I ignore the fact that they are making faces at each other as I search out the CD. I ignore the fact that Stephen is giggling and feeding the dog his oranges as I plug in the player. I insert the CD, push play, and somehow, through the magic of singing Christian vegetables, peace reigns once again. For a moment.

In the next minute, my two oldest children burst through the front door. "We're soaked!" they announce as they casually drop wet mittens by the door and leave a slushy trail through the living room, kicking boots in all directions. At that moment, Juliette and Ambrose commence a pushing fight over who gets to sit closest to the CD player, Stephen stands up in his high chair, leaning perilously over the edge, and I notice a smell of scorched hamburger coming from the stove. The cheerful voices of Bob the Tomato and Larry Cucumber fill the room as I race to remove the pan from the burner. Then, upon hearing a stomach-turning retch, I turn around to find the dog has vomited on the rug. Oranges.

I am no longer inspired. In fact, I am prepared to sit down next to the vomit and wallow in what I consider to be a fully-deserved moment of self-pity, when suddenly: Kick-kick! It is the smallest, quietest, and least demanding of my children who now gains my attention. This little person, not yet born, kicks and squirms and rolls. It's not so bad, his motions seem to tell me now. How bad can anything be when you have a little blessing like me hidden away in here? Encouraged by these thoughts, I put the dog outside, clean up the mess, and make macaroni for dinner.

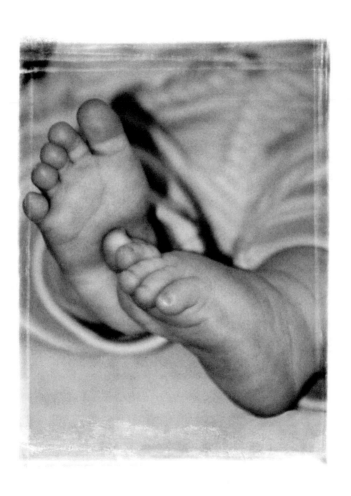

Days later, I am running late. Wet snow falls steadily and collects around the tires as I urge my mini-van along an unplowed road. My fingers grasp the steering wheel tightly as my glance alternates between the clock and my backseat passengers who are apparently unaware of our tardiness and the terrible driving conditions. I focus on keeping the van's tires within the faint snowy tracks before me, while in my mind I scold myself for not having left the house just a few minutes earlier. Why is it that no matter how organized I think I am, there is always one more shoe to find, one more trip to the bathroom, and one more face to wipe before we can go anywhere?

I am thinking these thoughts and wishing the weather would allow me to drive just a little bit faster, when suddenly: Kick-kick! It's Baby again. Without saying a word, he questions my priorities. Slow down, he admonishes. There isn't any place in the world you could be going that's more important than keeping me and the other children in this car safe. My littlest passenger is right, of course. I relax my grip on the steering wheel and slow down. We arrive at our destination predictably late, but thankfully unharmed.

As we are lying in bed early the next morning, Baby kicks hard against my husband's hand pressed against my belly. "Definitely a boy!" his father declares proudly. "He's trying to bust out of there!" Maybe this little one is a boy, but I don't think he is trying to get out. He is simply fulfilling the temporary role God has given him; he is my sweet, silent messenger from heaven.

14

Something's Got to Give

Balancing Work and Family Life
2004

Stephen wants juice.

"Juice, Mama!" he calls from the kitchen.

Working at the computer, I barely glance in his direction.

"In a minute, Sweetie."

After repeating his request a few times and not receiving a satisfactory response, he toddles over and waits patiently at my side. For about fifteen seconds.

"Juice, Mama..." he intones in his gravelly two-year-old voice.

I really want to finish proofreading an article, so without taking my eyes from the monitor, I scoop him onto my lap and smooth his hair.

Stephen will not be cuddled.

"No, Mama... Juice, Mama!"

He arches his back and wriggles from my arms. He marches to the refrigerator and hangs on the door handle.

"Juuuuuuuuuuuice... juuuuuuuuuuice... juuuuuuuuu-uuuice!"

"I'll be right there," I tell him.

Absorbed in my reading, I don't look up again until I hear something. Actually, the something I hear is nothing at all. As most mothers of two-year-olds know, a prolonged period of silence is nearly always cause for alarm.

I find Stephen sitting contentedly next to the open refrigerator in the kitchen. He no longer wants juice. His empty cup lies beside him and gripped in his grubby fingers is an almost empty can of frosting. His face, his hands, his hair, his shirt, and the kitchen tiles are smeared with Betty Crocker's creamy chocolate fudge.

Not only have I not finished my work, but now I have to clean the kitchen floor and scrub an obstinate Stephen before I can get back to it. These circumstances beg the question: Why didn't I just stop what I was doing and get him the darned juice in the first place?

The answer is because there is always juice to pour. By this I mean that there are always countless tiny tasks I could complete during the day instead of working on my writing. If I interrupt my work to pour Stephen's juice, I'll wipe up the counter before I leave the kitchen. Kateri will find me standing there and ask me to thread a needle or tie off her latest sewing project. Eamon will ask me how to spell "arthropod," I'll

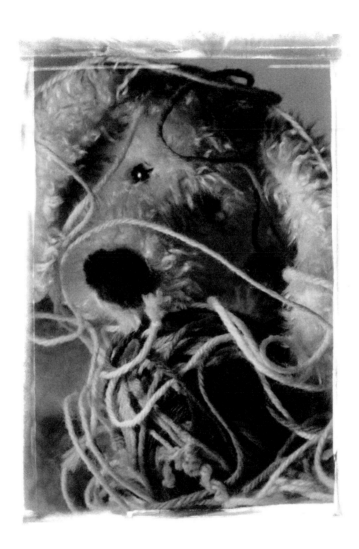

suddenly remember that I left a load of laundry in the dryer, and, as I hurry to fold T-shirts and match socks, the baby will wake up from her nap with a messy diaper and a crabby disposition.

One of the most common questions people ask me about working from home is, "How do you find the time?"

It can be a tricky balance. On some days, as I care for babies, homeschool older kids, keep up with laundry, prepare meals, and try to find time for my work, I can find myself near the breaking point. Something's got to give, I find myself thinking, and more often than not something does.

Some days it's dinner. Although I like to cook, I've been known to pop open cans of Spaghettios or serve up frozen pancakes when circumstances require a quick and easy meal. On other days it's the house that suffers. Once, near the end of a particularly time-consuming writing project, I took a bathroom break and discovered a toilet that looked like it belonged in a gas station and a sink smothering beneath a pile of dirty laundry.

While I am sometimes willing to give up elegant dinners and the ever-immaculate home of my dreams, I aim to ensure it's never my children who suffer at the hands of their multi-tasking mother.

Enter Dan.

My husband. My hero. He is the reason I am able to work from home without neglecting our children.

Lest anyone get the wrong idea, I don't mean that my darling spouse hurries home from work, dons a frilly apron, and prepares gourmet dinners while I pursue a glamorous writing career.

He does pour juice, though. He comes home during breaks in his school day to teach math lessons while I do laundry or read to preschoolers. He acquiesces uncomplainingly when I beg him to give me "just one hour" on the computer before we spend time together on a Saturday night. He also knows how to load the dishwasher, wipe a runny nose, and put on the baby's pajamas, and he does these things as needed.

Our family is a shared project. This busy life of ours works because we work at it together. As God intended, we smooth each other's rough spots and strengthen each other's weaknesses. Most importantly, we share responsibility for our home and children, each giving and taking as the circumstances demand.

Speaking of demanding circumstances, I am typing this with one hand as nine-month-old Gabrielle squirms in my lap and lunges for the keyboard. Stephen has abandoned a pile of toy trucks and is investigating the contents of my purse. Dan isn't due home for another few hours so I'll have to conclude this chapter some other—

15

What Little Girls Are Made Of

The Joy of the Unexpected
2002

When I was young and unmarried, I had a dream of having a daughter some day. My fantasy was a vague jumble of jump rope, lace-collared dresses, hair ribbons, and tea parties. I envisioned a little girl who wore braided pigtails and patent leather Mary Janes. Years later, when the doctor announced I had given birth to a girl, I felt unsure about many things, but fairly confident that at least I was entering familiar territory. After all, I was a little girl once. I knew what little girls were all about.

I am not sure exactly when reality checked my fantasy. Perhaps it was eighteen months later, when Kateri, my tow-headed toddler discovered grasshoppers. I was working in the garden when she returned from exploring the front lawn and presented me with chubby fists full of the hapless creatures. Their eyes were wide and staring. Their bodies crumpled in the clutches of her fat fingers. They covered her hands and her sweater sleeves with brown sticky fluid that oozed from their insect mouths.

"Ook! Mama! Ook! Ook!" she exclaimed with characteristic enthusiasm.

I shrieked, shook the grasshoppers from her hands, and rushed her into the house for a good scrubbing at the bathroom sink.

Kateri was undaunted. All that summer she continued to collect grasshoppers, as well as ants, beetles, moths, and spiders at every opportunity. She giggled with delight when a caterpillar crawled up her pant leg or a moth got lost in her hair. I squelched my own squeamishness and provided her with appropriate containers for her creepy, crawly catches. Somehow, without ever consciously thinking it, I had assumed my little girl would be just like me. Now, I watched her buggy activities with mixed emotions.

I didn't give up the idea, however, that my daughter would become the kind of little girl I once was. For her birthday, I searched toy stores and catalogs until I found the perfect doll, dressed in delicate floral pajamas. At first, Kateri humored me. She fed the doll a bottle and changed its diaper. It wasn't long, though, before she put the baby down for an extended nap. She put one of the dresses on a giant rubber grasshopper, her favorite birthday present, and soon "Hoppy" was accompanying us on every outing to the grocery store while the doll lay forgotten in her bassinet.

Countless times in the eight years since her birth, I have gazed at my daughter with wonder, this little girl who sports a backward baseball cap and roots for the St. Louis Rams with fierce emotion.

The ways in which our children surprise us can be a wonderful gift. They invite us to explore worlds we would never venture into on our own. They challenge assumptions we didn't even know we were making. Through them, God teaches us to accept and to love that which is vastly different from ourselves.

These days, Kateri has no time for tea parties, and fancy buckled shoes would only cramp her style. On summer mornings, she dons a pair of rubber boots and heads outdoors to explore the marshy edges of our property. I watch her faraway figure, silhouetted against the rising sun. She wades through thick mud and murky puddles carrying a metal pail that she fills with frogs, newts, salamanders, and giant water beetles. Sometimes she captures a garter snake and races home to show me her prize.

"Look!" she cries in breathless excitement as I back away from the wriggling reptile in her hands.

Her freckled nose is smudged with mud. Uncombed hair wildly frames her exuberant face. This little girl is no cookie-cutter, miniature version of myself. She never will be. She is unabashedly, irrepressibly, undeniably herself.

In other words, she is exactly what a little girl should be.

16

My Boy

Being a Faithful Child of God
2004

I have cooties. I don't mean to alarm anyone, but apparently it's true. The other night, when I tucked my five-year-old son Ambrose into bed, I leaned in to kiss him good night and was greeted with a stern, "Not on the lips, please."

Not on the lips? This is Ambrose, the same child I cherished and sang to during the months I carried him within me. I nursed him moments after his birth. I counted his fingers and toes and memorized every dimple and curve of his tiny, perfect body.

Not on the lips? As a toddler, Ambrose used to climb into my lap and beg, "Tickle love, Mama!" He then squealed with delight as I covered him with kisses and ravaged his belly with "raspberries."

Now, at five years old, perhaps in an effort to separate himself from the perceived weakness of "little boy" things, Ambrose has developed a sudden distaste for physical affection, particularly from his mother.

I am trying not to take it too personally. The first night I was admonished to avoid kissing his lips, I at first stood in stunned silence next to his bed. My maternal instincts told me to snatch his small body from the bed and clutch him close in spite of his protests. I resisted this urge, though. I swallowed my wounded pride and gently touched my lips to his cheek.

Some days, however, when he wrenches his hand away from mine or squirms his way out of a hug that lasts too long, I can't help but feel that this turn of events is terribly unfair. This is Ambrose, I think. I am his mother. He is *my* boy and I'll kiss him if I want to.

Eventually, though, I have to admit that although I am his mother, Ambrose is not mine. Whether I like it or not, he is fast becoming his own little person and he belongs to God alone. When I feel my little boy pulling away from me, my feelings of hurt and indignation make me realize all the more how much each of us owes to God.

"Before I formed you in the womb I knew you," God tells the prophet Jeremiah, "and before you were born, I consecrated you..." (Jer 1:5).

Indeed, God does know each of us perfectly. In perfect generosity he made us, and in perfect goodness he loves us unconditionally. More than anyone or anything on earth, our Creator has a claim on us. We belong to him. Despite this fact, however, God

doesn't force us to love him in return. Because he loves us, he gives us free will so that we might choose to know, love, and serve him. My hurt feelings at Ambrose's rejection make me recognize all the more what a grievous injustice it is for man to turn his back on his Creator and to deny God the devotion he deserves.

Recently, Ambrose and I spent a Saturday afternoon running errands together. We went to the drug store and the supermarket, and then stopped for a snack and a drink.

"This is fun," I told him. "It's like we're on a date."

When he asked what a date was, I explained that sometimes a boy and a girl go out together to have fun and get to know each other better. Keenly aware of his recent disdain for all things feminine, I teased him a little by telling him that someday he'll probably want to date a girl.

Ambrose nibbled an animal cracker thoughtfully. He was sober as he considered the concept of willingly spending free time with a member of the opposite sex.

If ever I doubted God's generous love and his tender care for even this humble mother's delicate feelings, my confidence was re-inspired by what Ambrose said next.

He fixed his gaze on me and said, "I want to date you, Mama."

I pulled my five-year-old boyfriend close so that he wouldn't see the tears in my eyes. I felt his small heart beating against my chest. I held him just a little bit longer than usual, and for now, he let me.

17

Martha, Martha

Balancing Daily Obligations and Prayer
2003

They shuffle along the aisles of the grocery store, oblivious to my frustrated presence behind them. Every few paces they pause. The old man pulls an item from the shelf and hands it to his wife who examines the label through thick-lensed glasses. Their cart blocks the aisle as they compare prices of canned corn. Together, they try to recall whether or not they are out of paper towels.

They are sweet but they are slow, and I, plodding along behind them with half a cartful of groceries and a toddler who is missing his nap, am growing impatient. I just want to pick up the few groceries I need, go to the post office, and get home in time to put my son down for his nap, finish the laundry, and make dinner before my oldest son's baseball game. I try unsuccessfully to maneuver my way around them. My son wriggles free of the grocery cart harness and scales my shoulder.

At times like these, when my head is filled with busy-ness, to-do lists, and growing frustration, I try to remind myself of the Gospel story of Christ's visit to the sisters, Mary and Martha. During his visit, Mary sits at Jesus' feet and listens intently to his teaching. Her sister Martha, however, is busy with the duties of a hostess—cooking, cleaning, and serving. When she complains to Jesus that Mary ought to be helping her, we can almost hear the amusement in our Lord's voice as he gently chides her: "...Martha, Martha, you are worried and distracted by many things; there is need of only one thing. Mary has chosen the better part, which will not be taken away from her." (Lk 10:41–42)

Poor Martha. She only wanted to receive her important guests properly. Even my mom, a veteran mother of nine and grandmother of twenty, laughs that Mary may have chosen the better part, but when all the talking was done they all were probably glad that someone had prepared dinner.

The lives of most wives and mothers are filled with the constant cares of daily living. The world needs us Martha-types to attend to these practical matters. There are children to bathe and floors to mop. There are meals to prepare and clothes to wash. Between work schedules, running errands, and meeting social obligations, it might seem like precious little time remains in which to accomplish all the housekeeping chores that must be done. We Marthas, however, must keep in mind that

ultimately these things are not what is most important. If we are not careful, our tasks can consume us.

I need to remind myself regularly that my ultimate goal is getting myself and my family to heaven. The chores involved in keeping us clean, organized, and well fed in the meantime are not nearly so important. When our Lord said, "There is need of only one thing," he surely was not referring to scrubbing the bathroom tiles, picking up the dry cleaning, or even getting all the laundry done by dinnertime, however miraculous that might be. It can be easy to forget in the course of our active lives, but the tasks which fill our days are not the "better part." Our spiritual life is. Martha was so preoccupied with practical matters that she missed Christ in her living room. What might we be missing?

With the proper perspective, finding myself stuck behind an elderly couple at the grocery store becomes an occasion to practice patience. Perhaps it's not vital that there be a check mark next to every item on my list of things to do today. I might benefit from slowing down a bit.

That evening, after the older kids have gone to bed, I sit on the couch to nurse my newborn daughter. If I check, I will notice that the floor beneath my feet needs sweeping. If I look, I will see that a pile of dirty dishes awaits me in the kitchen sink. But I don't check and I don't look. Instead, I examine Gabrielle's miniature fingers clenched in a tiny, perfect fist. I note her expression of complete contentment as she nestles in the crook of my arm. I kiss her soft, bald head and offer God the spontaneous prayer of thanksgiving that bursts forth from my heart.

18

Mass Distraction

Worshipping with Babies

2002

Stephen pulls at the neckline of my sweater. His tiny, wet fingers explore my ears and neck. He grabs a fistful of my hair and stuffs it into his mouth. I keep my eyes forward, silently congratulating myself for paying attention to the first reading despite the antics of my seven-month-old sidekick. When I glance at the missal over my husband's shoulder, however, I discover that I am actually listening to the second reading. How could that be? What was the first reading? Did I really miss the Psalm?

I pick up my own missal to refresh my memory. As I flip through the pages, the crinkle of paper attracts Stephen's attention and he lunges toward the book. I try to hold it out of his reach, but he whines in frustration, so instead I close the missal and put it away. His whine turns into a wail. When I try to silence him with a pacifier, he slaps it from my hand and shrieks with rage. A few people in the front pew turn around to look at us. My husband grimaces.

I smile apologetically, squeeze past my older children sitting in the pew, and begin a familiar walk down the aisle toward the back of the church. Most people avert their eyes. A few older ladies smile at my screeching bundle. Children crane their necks to watch us walk past.

"Where's Mama going?" I hear the sound of my two-year-old's voice above the Alleluia.

So it is another Sunday morning, and I am exiled once again. I stand at the back of the church, balancing Stephen on my hip. He clings to me like a tiny monkey, and at last he is quiet. I sometimes wonder about the kind of spiritual life God expects me to have when I find it difficult even to pay attention while I am at Mass. With young children occupying my days and nights, it seems that attending an uninterrupted Mass once a week would be a minimal request. I find some comfort, though, in knowing I am not the only parent with a far from contemplative spiritual life.

"Let's put it this way," my sister joked in a recent phone conversation, "I'm not in danger of levitating any time soon."

The other outcasts I meet at the back of the church each Sunday also appear to have their feet planted firmly on the ground. We share knowing glances as we rock boisterous babies in our arms. We exchange apologies and nods of understanding when

the toddlers we are chasing happen to collide. We wave to each other's children at the sign of peace.

An older woman once stopped me after Mass and told me not to be embarrassed by Stephen's disturbances.

"He gives glory to God by being the best baby he can be," she explained.

I think she was right. Babies may not sit peacefully in the pews worshipping God as grown-ups do, but they praise God in the only way they can, by being the beautiful creatures he intended them to be. They don't waste time wondering about God's expectations or longing for different circumstances. They whole-heartedly embrace the role they have been given. Every squirming, drooling, grabbing, shrieking inch of these little ones testifies to the glory and wonder of God's creation.

Perhaps we parents who are distracted by their pawing hands and active bodies can learn from their example. Just as Stephen's job is to be a baby, mine is to be his mother. Like a flower that blooms where it is planted, I give glory to God if I embrace the role he has chosen for me. God doesn't want me to levitate. He wants me to give my little ones the attention they require, even when it's inconvenient, even when it seems there are holier things to do. I cannot easily follow the readings or meditate on the sermon while at Mass, but I can unconditionally accept the tasks God gives me right now, on this particular Sunday morning.

Sometimes accepting God's will means getting up in the middle of the night for nightmares or drinks of water. Sometimes it means cutting a phone call short to break up a squabble.

This morning it means attending Mass from the back of the church while trying to keep Stephen from ripping the earrings from my earlobes. There is spit-up on my sweater. The baby writhes and wriggles in my arms. I smile indulgently as he tears a barrette from my hair and waves it triumphantly above his head, squealing with delight. Glory be to God!

19

Less Than Perfect

Praying As a Family

2004

Things usually start out smoothly enough. Each evening, my husband and I sit on the couch with six pajama-clad children beside us, around us, and in our laps. We help the littlest ones make a sign of the cross and then together we recite the same words I used to pray with my parents each night:

"Thank you God for my happy day..."

Then the interruptions begin.

"What if my day wasn't happy?" Ambrose wants to know.

"There's something happy about every day," I assure him, but he is not satisfied.

"No, really. What if you fell down and hit your head and had to go to the hospital and get a shot and then you broke your favorite toy?"

"Then you should be happy that you survived and grateful for the doctors who took care of you at the hospital."

Ambrose looks like he wants to argue his point further, but when he sees the stern expression on my face he decides against it.

"Take care of me tonight," we continue. "I'm sorry if I did something wrong today..."

This time Juliette is curious.

"Do we do something wrong every day?" she asks. "I don't think I did anything wrong today."

"Of course you did," her older sister Kateri chimes in. "Remember how you took away the book that Stephen was looking at and then threw it when Mama told you to give it back?"

Her words invite more children to contribute their thoughts about the wrongdoings of others and before I know it family prayer time has dissolved into a one-upping game of accusations and tattle-taling. So much for heavenly perfection!

Attempting to say the rosary as a family can be even more challenging. The baby is usually distracted by the beads, but unfortunately so are the other children.

"Which one are we on?" they ask in not-so-quiet whispers throughout each decade.

"Is this the right one?" they demand as they thrust their rosaries in our faces.

The more reserved ones try to catch my eye and then gesture wildly and point at their beads with exaggerated bewildered expressions.

Let's face it. Family prayer time, particularly with small children, is usually less than perfect, and saying the rosary can be especially complicated. Reciting the prayers, keeping track of the beads, and meditating on the mysteries often requires more mental and physical coordination than the average child possesses. Ultimately, in the face of endless distractions and continual disruptions, it can be tempting to abandon regular prayer time with children.

We could never give it up, though. One of my favorite parts of family prayer time is when we give each child an opportunity to speak his or her mind, petitioning God for favors and thanking him for special blessings. Their words in these moments give us a rare look into their innermost thoughts and feelings. Kateri thanks God for mud puddles and the frogs that live in them. Eamon asks God to bless a thoughtful woman at church who occasionally surprises our children with little gifts. Juliette asks God to help all the mothers in the world who have babies in their bellies. Through their own words we learn what they value most and discover their personal concerns, and that is precious to me.

Most important, however, is the example we set for our children when we pray together as a family. When we persist in gathering for daily prayers despite innumerable obstacles, our actions demonstrate the importance of prayer in a way that our words never could.

In particular, I find Dan's participation in our family prayer life especially valuable. In our children's estimation—at least so far—there is no more authoritative or commanding person in the world than their father. When they witness their "hero" kneeling before God, expressing gratitude, and asking for help, they recognize the supremacy of God. Without his father's example, a young boy might all too easily conclude that faith and prayer are feminine or childish things. Dan's example demonstrates to our boys in particular that an active prayer life and deep devotion to God are essential components of manhood.

When prayer time becomes exasperating, it helps to remind myself that when it comes to prayer, it truly is the thought that counts. Even when two-year-old Stephen tires of the rosary and strips off his pajamas to amuse his older siblings, we are trying very hard to pray, and our sincere efforts are pleasing to God.

We might not say a flawless family rosary until Stephen is in college. We might never say one. The point is, though, that we are praying. Just as a loving parent would never reject a small child's imperfect attempt to say, "I love you," our Father and Mother in heaven will not be offended by our well-intentioned prayerful blunders.

"We wuv you," we tell them and they love us back.

20

Nesting Is for the Birds

The Blessings of Maternal Instinct
2004

Dust bunnies lurk behind my living room couch. My stovetop never seems to sparkle quite like my mother's. Usually, Labor Day finds me still planning to get around to my "spring cleaning."

For these reasons, it was with particular interest that I learned about the so-called "nesting syndrome" when I was expecting my first child. Apparently, my books told me, just as a mother bird prepares a nest for her impending brood, a human mother sometimes will experience bursts of energy and an urge to clean her surroundings in the final weeks of pregnancy. This instinct, some theorize, is nature's way of preparing a clean and suitable home for the new baby.

I was fascinated by the idea that I might actually become a praiseworthy housekeeper during the upcoming months. Would wild hormones really render me capable of achieving the organized kitchen cabinets, immaculate toilet bowl, and dust-free windowsills of my dreams? I watched my growing belly with increasing wonder as the months passed.

When I was eight months along, the weight of my pregnancy began to take its toll on me. On some days, when fatigue overwhelmed me, I would re-read the paragraphs in my baby books which described the "nesting syndrome" and wonder if it could be real. At the end of a long day, when I found myself gasping for breath after a walk to the mailbox, when the thought of folding a single load of laundry made me want to cry, it seemed unlikely that my pregnant body would ever be up to the task of "nesting."

As my due date approached, my older, more-experienced sister suggested that I give my bathroom a thorough scrubbing before the baby was born. "After the baby," she warned in a wise older-sister tone, "you'll have trouble finding time to brush your teeth."

Not long afterward, I found myself alone at home during a day off from work. I remembered my sister's advice and decided she was probably right. Reluctantly, I pulled out my stash of cleaners and tackled the bathroom.

Then it happened. Somewhere between scrubbing mildew from the shower tiles and polishing the chrome fixtures, I became an unwitting victim of nature.

The smell of bleach invigorated me. My sparkling bathtub inspired me. I finished the bathroom and pulled out the vacuum cleaner. When straight, perfect

vacuum lines appeared on the carpet, I moved on to the bedroom.

I gathered dirty T-shirts from the floor, and started a load of laundry. I windexed the windows and went for the furniture polish. When the woodwork shone, I organized my sock drawer. I systematically emptied, dusted, and refilled the linen closet with stacks of neatly folded sheets and towels.

I moved swiftly from one task to the next. My energy seemed boundless. I had no heartburn. I had no Braxton Hicks contractions. I had no achy varicose veins or shortness of breath. Without pause, I folded, dusted, scrubbed, polished, tidied, freshened, straightened, arranged, swept, and wiped.

Hours later, when my husband came home from work, he found me in a spotless kitchen, organizing the spice rack. He looked around our lemon-scented home in astonishment and then looked to me for an explanation.

Something about the look on his face jarred me from my frenzied bout of housecleaning. As I listed the chores that I had completed and explained the urgency behind dusting the light fixtures, I awoke from my hormonal haze. The words of my baby books' descriptions of "nesting syndrome" came back to me and I put down my dust cloth.

So it was real. I had spent my day satisfying an instinctual urge to prepare a home for my baby. Like a proud mama bird, I looked over my gleaming nest and suddenly realized that I hadn't eaten lunch. My shoulders ached. My legs throbbed. I was out of breath and desperate to sit down. I made my way across the vacuum lines to the living room couch and propped my back against a freshly plumped pillow.

As I lay there reeling from my "nesting syndrome" hangover, I wondered about the practicality of such an instinct. Would the cobwebs in the far corners of the hall closet really have posed a threat to my newborn baby? How would the fact that I had alphabetized my old college notebooks benefit an infant? Would my baby even notice the absence of dust on the blades of the ceiling fan?

During each of my following five pregnancies, I have eagerly anticipated the "nesting syndrome," and usually I have not been disappointed. In a household full of kids, however, cleanliness is a temporary thing. I have often had to settle for just getting the laundry caught up and the kitchen counters wiped down before heading to the hospital for a new delivery.

On that fateful day during my first pregnancy, though, my home was immaculate, but my body felt abused and I despaired at the thought of making dinner. I groaned and rubbed my stiffened neck. Helplessly, I looked at my hungry, bewildered husband.

Fortunately, papa birds have some useful instincts of their own. My devoted mate admired our nest, smoothed my feathers, and took me out for dinner.

21

Mom Olympics
All Mothers Are Champions
2003

I had a brief career in soccer when I was seven years old and the only girl on my older brother's team. My most vivid memory is of the absolute panic which overcame me once when the ball was accidentally kicked in my direction.

"Kick it!" I heard my father yell from the sidelines, and so I did kick it, more to get it (and the ensuing mob of eight-year-old boys) away from me than anything else. I quit the team soon after and reclaimed my Saturday mornings for more important things, like jumprope and Scooby Doo.

Just because I was not destined for stardom on the soccer field, though, does not mean that I have no athletic aspirations. We are all teammates of a sort, using our individual talents and working to further God's kingdom on earth. I have always thought that mothers in particular have specialized athletic skills. Perhaps if there were a "Mom Olympics" these would be better recognized...

First Event: Laundry!

In this event, the mom runs up a flight of stairs holding a screaming fifteen-pound baby in one arm and a full basket of laundry in the other, leaps over a safety gate at the top, and answers the telephone before the caller hangs up.

Second Event: Road Trip!

Now the mom drives a minivan containing an assortment of small children. She quickly and completely meets the needs of her backseat passengers while maintaining safety on the road. This may require serving juice, finding the baby's pacifier, breaking up a spitting fight, or even killing a spider. A point penalty will be assessed for turning up the radio to drown out their demands.

Third Event: Supermarket!

Now the mom pushes a grocery cart (with assorted children attached) through the crowded aisles of a major supermarket. Without giving in to their pleas for various forms of sugar, she prevents the children from breaking or stealing any merchandise. She completes a shopping list for a week's worth of groceries, reading labels, watching for specials, and remembering her husband's favorite brand of frozen french fries.

Fourth Event: Dinner!

In this event the Mom prepares a delicious, nutritious, well-balanced meal for her family. Obstacles include a whiny two-year-old climbing the cabinets, a

ringing telephone, and a four-year-old who is "helping" by unfolding the laundry and spreading it on the dining room table. Points are deducted for overcooking the broccoli, but extra points are awarded for convincing a preschooler to eat it.

Fifth Event: Bedtime!

Now the mom bathes an assortment of indefatigable little people, removing chewing gum from their hair, sand from their ears, and spaghetti sauce from their faces. She brushes their teeth, wrestles them into pajamas, and finds a bedtime story which is approved by children of three different age levels. She tucks them in their beds while satisfactorily answering the questions which naturally arise at this time of day, such as, "Who made God?" and, "How exactly does a baby get in its mommy's belly?"

I know the competition would be stiff, but, with my daily training, I feel fairly confident that I could earn a medal in the "Mom Olympics." My picture might appear on Wheaties boxes with a baby on my hip and a plastic sippy cup raised triumphantly above my head. On early morning television, Matt Lauer might interview me about my training regimen and my diet of peanut butter and jelly.

When I arrived home from swimming lessons this morning, however, Matt Lauer was nowhere in sight. No reporters accosted me on my way to the front door to ask how I survived the perils of a morning at the lake with small children.

I realize that there may never be a "Mom Olympics" and, believe it or not, that's okay with me. When my frenzied days of mothering come to an end, I only hope that like St. Paul, I too will be able to say, "I have fought the good fight, I have finished the race, I have kept the faith" (2 Tim 4:7).

22

A Winning Combination

Contrasting Perspectives on Competition
2004

My husband Dan's eyes glazed over during our childbirth instructor's explanation of dilation and effacement. He wasn't exactly a natural at rhythmic breathing and foot massages. When he learned that he was to be my labor coach as I prepared to give birth to our first child, however, his eyes lit up. Coaching was most definitely something he could do.

Dan has always been an athlete, and a driven one at that. As a part-time high school tennis coach years ago, he was happiest on the tennis court with a clipboard under his arm and a whistle around his neck. During practice, his young charges snapped to attention at the sound of his whistle. Before matches they huddled eagerly around him to hear his soft-spoken words of encouragement before storming the courts with confidence and enthusiasm. If I needed someone to coach me through childbirth, then Dan was the man to do it.

A few weeks before the baby was due, he sat me down for a pep talk.

"The way I see it is this," he said, "it's near the end of the season and we're in this to win. Things will probably get messy in there, but we're going to push through the pain. It's called winning ugly. It won't be pretty, but we'll get the job done."

"We're having a baby not a basketball," I told him.

As much as seeing childbirth as a competitive event was helpful to Dan, I could not appreciate the analogy. It's a male-female thing. Back when I used to run on the track team in high school, my male teammates were somber and focused before a race, meeting their opponents' eyes with icy stares. We girls, however, would gather at the starting line amidst a jumble of apologies and self-deprecating remarks.

"No one needs to worry about me," one girl would say, "I stink."

"Oh no, I'm sure you don't!" another would respond. "I'm really terrible!"

"Why doesn't someone else take the inside lane?" a third would offer. "I don't want to get in the way."

Although I have always accepted and even admired Dan's competitive determination, I was apprehensive when I noticed some of the same tendencies in our children, especially the boys. As they grew, it seemed that board games, hide-and-seek, and even races to their beds too frequently ended in tears

once the "winners" and "losers" were determined. The day I returned from a baby shower and Eamon asked, "Did you win?" I knew I needed to address the situation.

Hoping to encourage family teamwork and solidarity, I made a trip to the library and returned with a stack of books about cooperative games for children. Most of them were printed in the 1970s and featured photographs of shaggy-haired, bell-bottomed children holding hands and making "shoe salads." When he saw what I was reading, Dan rolled his eyes and worried aloud that his wife might be turning "hippie" on him.

If the outdated photographs and my husband's reservations didn't dissuade me, the children's reaction to playing "Human Popcorn" did. After crouching on the floor and pretending to be corn kernels simmering in oil, they "popped" and bounced around the room, knocking down a lamp and tripping over the dog. After a few minutes of chaos, they grew bored with just bouncing and started bouncing and bumping one another. When that got old, they started bouncing, bumping, and pushing. Eventually, a big popcorn kernel pushed a little popcorn kernel who fell to the floor and burst into tears. Above the noise of laughter, crying, and the dog barking, I shouted at them to stop "popping."

Dejectedly, they looked at me and asked, "Is that the end of the game?"

"Yes," I told them. "That was cooperative enough."

Kids aren't dummies. Even if we moms try to convince them their T-Ball games all end in ties, they know the score. The key is to avoid extremes in either direction, and that's why God made fathers and mothers. The differences between Dan and I complement each other. Between his competitiveness and my cooperation, our children find balance.

A couple of times a week Dan takes the children and some of their friends to the gym to coach them in basketball, and they usually end their lessons with a race across the gymnasium. The children line up at the starting line, poised and ready. At the sound of Dan's whistle they explode in a sprint toward the other side.

"C'mon, Eamon, push it! Faster, Ambrose!" Dan shouts.

I stand on the sidelines quietly encouraging and applauding everyone's efforts.

"Good job, everybody!"

With the combined support of both parents, when at last they cross the finish line, everyone is a winner.

23

Baking Lessons

Letting Go of Perfectionism
2001

$\mathcal{I}$t beckons to me from the slick, sophisticated pages of a gourmet cooking magazine. The pastry is golden brown with a perfectly fluted edge. Juicy fruit filling bubbles beneath a meticulously woven top crust. The accompanying article suggests that my family deserves a freshly baked peach pie and promises that I can reproduce this masterpiece in my own kitchen with a few simple ingredients. I want to believe it. I am determined to try it. I clip the recipe and add peaches to my grocery list.

Early the next morning I push up my sleeves, gather my ingredients and pulling out my rolling pin. Looking at the pile of peaches on my kitchen counter, I envision myself baking a beautiful pie with the same lattice crust and bubbly filling I saw in the magazine. Of course, in fantasies we tend to gloss over the minor details. In this case, one of those minor details is Juliette, my late-night-teething ten-month-old who has turned into an exhausted-early-morning-whiner and is desperately clinging to my leg as I attempt to blanch the peaches.

"Poor baby," I try to comfort her. I pat her head and smooth her fine, blonde baby hair. She holds fast to my leg. I maintain my lattice-topped fantasy, however, as I limp, baby and all, from stove, to sink, to counter, blanching, peeling, pitting, and slicing.

"Mama! I wanna see!" two-year-old Ambrose calls above the sound of his sister's whining. Another minor detail. I make room for the chair he is pushing up to the counter and continue blanching, peeling, pitting, and slicing.

When just a few peaches remain to be sliced, Juliette realizes that I am ignoring her and suddenly despairs of ever being picked up again. Her whine becomes a high-pitched wail. Ambrose covers his ears with his hands. I scoop up the baby and balance her on one hip while I slice peaches with the other hand. She breathes a loud sigh and rests her head against my chest.

The peace lasts only a moment, though, as I try frantically to finish slicing. Juliette notices the peaches. A large bowl filled with shiny, freshly-sliced fruit proves irresistible. She lunges forward, grabs a slice, and greedily stuffs it into her mouth. It had not previously occurred to her older brother to try such a daring maneuver, but when he sees her get away with it, he grabs a slice too. He flashes me a look of delight at his own naughtiness and pops it into his mouth.

"That's enough," I warn, slicing madly. "Now you've each had a taste, but I need the rest for the pie. No more."

Of course, a baby does not understand such an instruction, and a two-year-old often chooses to ignore instructions of any kind, so the scene that follows involves a great deal of reaching, whining, and grabbing on their parts, and admonishing, threatening, and bribing on mine. In the end, each of them has eaten several pieces of fruit, but the slicing is done.

I place the bowl of sliced peaches out of their reach and measure out the flour and shortening for the pie crust. Juliette wriggles from my arms and onto the counter. She peers into the mixing bowl and thrusts both hands into the flour. I immediately pull out her hands and clap them together to dust off the flour. This produces little dust clouds that she and her brother find terribly amusing. Now they both reach into the bowl, clap their hands, and erupt in fits of giggles.

"No!" I scold them firmly. I push their hands from the mixing bowl, consult the recipe, retrieve my measuring spoons from Juliette's mouth, and somehow manage to finish mixing the dough.

Next, I sprinkle some flour onto the counter, plop the dough on top, and proceed to smooth it with the rolling pin. Ambrose pokes at the dough with one finger and tastes a bit from the edge. I ignore this minor

infraction. Juliette, however, is not so subtle. Shame-lessly, she grabs a fistful of dough and bites into it.

"Mmmmmm..." she announces her approval.

I remember the magnificent pie in the magazine as I consider the mess on my counter. I begin to think it will be impossible to produce a comparable pie in my kitchen. I clench my jaw. Perhaps a mother of young children has no business reading fancy cooking maga-zines. Maybe perfect pies are produced only in the pris-tine, childless kitchens of magazine food editors. I am quite certain that professional chefs never have to work under these conditions. As I ponder these facts, Ambrose reaches for the pastry cutter.

"STOP!" I finally snap. "Stop touching!"

My voice is an ugly sound. Ambrose's hand halts in midair. His eyebrows pinch together in a look of gen-uine bewilderment. His eyes penetrate mine for a moment, then he lets his hand fall, scrunches up his mouth, and asks, "Why?"

His earnest expression disarms me. I am jarred from my frenzied pursuit of the perfect pie as I pause to consider things from his perspective. I realize that my results-oriented approach to making a pie makes no sense to a child. Ambrose revels in the glorious sight of a bowl of sliced peaches gleaming like jewels in the sunlight. He wants to taste them right now and let their sweet juice dribble down his chin. Who cares if they are ever made into a pie? Ambrose doesn't know much about lattice crusts either, but he delights in the satiny smooth feel of rolled-out pie dough and relishes its squish between his fingers. Why shouldn't he touch? I have been so eager to finish making a perfect pie that I have forgotten what pleasures there are in the process.

I let go of my perfect pie fantasy. Juliette sits contentedly on the counter as Ambrose helps me roll out the remaining pie dough. Along the way, we sprinkle flour like snow onto the kitchen floor. We stamp our sweatshirts with white handprints. Leftover bits of dough become balls and snakes and snails. Then we breathe the sweet smell of peaches as we mix them with sugar. We enjoy their slippery feel and sample their sticky syrup.

In the end, the pie I pull from the oven hardly resembles the beauty I saw in the cooking magazine. Its fluted edge is too dark and a bit lopsided. The plain top crust is uneven and slightly sunken in the center. I have not recreated a masterpiece as I had planned. Instead, I have spent the morning enjoying simple pleasures with my children. As any two-year-old will tell you, sometimes achieving perfect results is not as important as savoring special moments together. The pie doesn't look great, but it will probably taste pretty good.

Besides, when I thank Ambrose for his help, his smile is delicious.

24

For Better or for Worse

The Give and Take of Married Life
2003

There is a twelve-inch compound miter saw in my living room. With an eye to our springtime remodeling plans, my husband bought this piece of equipment, as well as the metal table it sits on, shortly after Christmas. That evening, I naively helped him carry it into the house and set it up in the living room where he assured me it would remain "for only a day."

In my husband's defense, I must admit that he got a good deal on the saw and that we currently lack adequate storage for such a large item; but in my defense, I must point out that he said "only a day," and it has been much more than a day. In fact, it has been many, many days, and I am growing weary of vacuuming around the saw, retrieving toys from underneath it, and explaining its presence to visitors.

In my weaker moments, I recall our wedding day and I am certain that none of the vows I took that day made mention of power equipment in the living room.

I suppose, however, that the saw is in those vows somewhere, perhaps falling under that sneaky, catch-all phrase, "for better or for worse." I am continually surprised by the particulars that make up the "worse." On the positive side, though, I am just as often surprised by the things that make up the "better."

Before we were married, my husband and I promised each other that we would never become one of those unromantic married couples with which we were all too familiar. We were young; we envisioned a marital life filled with passionate moments, fresh-cut flowers, and candle-lit dinners. We did our share of those things, but today, many years and quite a few children later, I no longer anticipate flowers and chocolates when my husband returns from work. I am delighted if he remembers the gallon of milk I asked him to bring home. Am I missing out? Am I deprived? I don't think so.

Over the years, my husband, who is a teacher, has gotten up before the sun and stayed up long past dark working a variety of different part-time and summer jobs to ensure that our family is always well provided for. He has been a coach, a golf course groundskeeper, and a waiter. He has worked fourteen-hour days tearing apart old barns to salvage materials and build our home. His diligence and dedication to our family's welfare are a part of the "better" I never could have anticipated years ago.

There are other parts, too. Like many mothers, I sometimes find myself feeling particularly unfulfilled

by my duties of squelching squabbles, wiping noses, and cleaning up the eternal messes that are part of an active household. On these days, when he calls home from work, my husband can tell by the sound of my voice that today would be a good day to bring home a pint of Ben & Jerry's "Super Fudge Chunk" and put the kids to bed early. His demonstrations of kindness and compassion when I am having a bad day are another unexpected part of the "better."

Then there are the days when we meet in the midst of chaos. Small children squawk in our arms, large children argue over whose turn it is to clear the table, the dog races through the room toppling a chair, and stuffed animals fly through the air from unknown origins.

At these times, when our eyes meet across the unruly room, my husband mouths the words, "I can't wait until two hours from now." I have to smile. In two hours, in a more orderly home filled with sleeping children, we will enjoy the grown-up pleasure of peace and quiet. Our shared moments of calm in the midst of the storm of family life and its daily demands are a part of the "better" I never would have appreciated as a young bride.

As our relationship matures, I discover that marriage is filled with the unexpected. I never thought being a faithful wife would mean tolerating a power saw in my living room. When we accommodate these unexpected trials, however, we make room for other surprises, more wonderful than we could have imagined. This kind of marriage is not a romance of the typical hearts and flowers variety. It's better.

25

A Reluctant Messenger

Living out Christian Duty

2004

I suppose there are worse things our parish's religious education director could have asked me to do. The day he asked me to substitute-teach a CCD class of eighth graders, though, it didn't feel that way. He probably dared to ask such an enormous favor because he happens to be my husband. He also happened to have just finished picking up the living room and offering to make the kids' dinner when he made his outrageous request.

Dan was conveniently forgetting that the class he was hoping I would cover was the same one whose teacher had just quit. It was also the same one Dan had taught the previous week. Discouraged, he had come home and announced, "They're all boys and every one of them has a behavior problem."

As a mother of six, I can weather a fair amount of abuse. But eighth grade boys? I didn't even like eighth grade boys when I was an eighth grade girl. In particular, I remember the boys in my eighth grade CCD class years ago. Miss Goddard, a soft-spoken college student with aspirations for the convent was their hapless victim. I am sure that quiet kids like me who sat in the front row were her sole consolation.

If my husband, who makes his living teaching adolescent boys, had difficulty controlling this particular class, what exactly did he expect me to accomplish with this rowdy bunch?

As a mother and teacher of grade-school children, I revel in felt-board Bible stories and sticker prizes for memorizing prayers. These teenagers, I was certain, would eat me alive.

Despite my protests, Dan assured me that these particular hooligans might respond positively to a female teacher. He took the baby from my arms, handed me my coat, and ushered me out the door.

I drove to the church with trepidation, then I stood in the doorway of the classroom feeling even smaller than my five-foot, one-inch frame. I said a quick prayer, took a deep breath, and stepped inside.

As soon as I walked in, Joshua, a freckle-faced boy wearing a backward baseball cap, leaped from his seat and let out a whoop.

"Yes!" he shouted, pumping his fist in the air. "It's not Mr. Bean—I hated Mr. Bean!"

"Dude," one of his friends interrupted his victory dance, "that's Mrs. Bean."

Jesus loves you!

Joshua's fist froze in mid-air. Color filled his face as he slunk into his chair and his classmates exploded with laughter. We were off to a roaring start.

I'd like to report that there were no problems as we took turns reading from the text and answering questions that evening, but of course that wouldn't be true. I endured some obnoxious noises, ignored some pencil-poking antics, and confiscated two packs of gum, a motorbike magazine, and a Gameboy. We managed to complete the chapter, though, and I think a couple of those kids actually listened when I described the gifts of the Holy Spirit.

My moderate successes started me thinking. Doesn't Our Lord's message speak to these boys in their droopy jeans and oversized sneakers? In spite of their tough attitudes and disruptive behavior, doesn't our faith belong to them too? When Christ told us, "Go into all the world and proclaim the good news to the whole creation" (Mk 16:15), he did not offer the option of skipping over those who are uncooperative or reluctant to hear what we have to say. He never said to spread the good news only among polite, pleasant people who make us feel comfortable and welcome.

At the end of class, the boys joked and jostled as they shuffled from the room. They were still foreign creatures to me, but they seemed somehow less intimidating than before.

Joshua lingered by my desk for a moment.

"Who's gonna teach us next week?" he asked. I shrugged my shoulders and told him I didn't know who his new teacher would be. After he left, though, I had to admit that I did know.

It would be me.

26

Continual Commitment

Daily Challenges of Teaching at Home
2004

*W*hen my first child was a baby, I waited breathlessly for her to learn my name.

"Did you hear that?" I squealed to my husband after many patient months. "She clearly said 'Mama,' and I think she was looking at me. Do you suppose she means it?"

I might not have been so thrilled if I had realized that once kids start saying "Mama," they don't stop. With the many children in our household, I get dozens of "Mamas" every day.

Some are sweet, like when baby Gabrielle, delighted to see me after waking up from her nap, sighs, "Mama," and rests her tiny head against my chest. Some are bloodcurdling, like the time four-year-old Eamon, after stepping on a wasps' nest while out walking in our field, shrieked, "Mamaaaaaaa...!"

Others are just plain exasperating, like the ones that assault me some mornings as I sit at the dining room table and attempt to complete morning lessons with the children.

"Mama," Kateri whines. "Do I hafta do all of these division problems? I already know how to do division." The margins of her worksheet are filled with cartoon doodles. "Mama," Eamon interjects. "This says to underline the nouns but I have no idea what that means." We did a lesson on nouns two days ago, but it has apparently flushed from his memory.

"Mama," Ambrose jumps in with a hopeless expression on his face. "I know I'm supposed to practice letters, but I can't find my handwriting book anywhere!" Ambrose, a creative and charming child, is notoriously absent-minded. I once sent him to retrieve a bag of groceries from the car and he managed to misplace it somewhere between the car and the kitchen.

"Mama!" Juliette howls from the living room. "Stephen is stealing my babies!"

"I not, Mama," two-year-old Stephen protests through his pacifier as he rips a doll from his sister's hands. "It mine."

I think I feel the "Mamas" most acutely because we are a homeschooling family.

When people find out that we homeschool our children, they sometimes ask, "How do you always give them all the attention they need?"

The fact is, it isn't always possible, and some homeschooling days are just plain overwhelming.

When our oldest was still a baby, I visited an acquaintance once, a homeschooling mother of seven. When I entered her living room, I held my baby close and watched the uproar in quiet astonishment. The uncontrolled atmosphere scandalized me. Her house was overflowing with plastic toys, dirty dishes, baskets of laundry, and what seemed like thousands of noisy children.

Mostly, I think I was terrified that I might become that woman. Dan and I had talked about homeschooling and I was open to the idea, but as I watched that wild-haired, sweatpants-wearing woman drowning in the midst of chaos, I remember thinking, "May that never be me."

On particularly bad days, when I feel like I am drowning in piles of schoolwork, housework, and children, I recall that poor harried woman and I cringe to think what a young new mother might think if she stepped into my house. On these days, it can be tempting to hurl my kids onto the nearest school bus and be done with it.

Like marriage, I have found that persevering in home education requires daily commitment and continual effort. On rough days, I try to keep in mind the reasons we chose homeschooling in the first place. One of the main benefits is that we spare our children exposure to a host of negative influences in public schools, but there are other unexpected advantages as well.

For example, I believe that one of the most precious blessings of homeschooling is that it helps me to maintain a close relationship with each of my children. By not turning them over to the care of other adults for a large part of each day, we gain valuable time with them. I like to think that this increases the likelihood that I will be the one my children turn to with their most intimate problems and important questions. When Kateri has questions about the sacraments and when Eamon worries about what he will be when he grows up—I want to be there for those "Mamas."

There are others I don't want to miss either. One recent stormy afternoon found all of us gathered on the couch indulging in a giant pile of favorite children's books. Even the older children listened with rapt attention as I read "Curious George Bakes a Cake" and our beloved "Peter Rabbit," complete with animated voices and dramatic pauses in all the right places. When I closed the last book, all of us sat quietly for a moment savoring the cozy warmth of each other's bodies and listening to the rhythm of raindrops against the windows. Juliette snuggled in close and wrapped her arms around my neck.

"Mama," she said. "I just like being here."

I reflected on the worn-out woman of my memory and decided that, despite outward appearances, she probably didn't have it so bad after all. Neither do I.

27

The Pumpkin Connection
Celebrating Oktoberfest
2004

On a warm September afternoon the children are seated at the kitchen table with piles of crayons and stacks of paper. Their heads are bent so intently over their work that they scarcely notice me as I breeze through with a basket of laundry.

I glance over Ambrose's shoulder to see a lopsided pumpkin with untamed hair and a wild smirk. Eamon is absorbed in his own drawing of an angry Jack-o'-Lantern with sharp, pointed eyebrows. Kateri's unpretentious pumpkin grins through gapped teeth.

"How many days is it now, Mama?" Ambrose asks.

You might think my children are eagerly anticipating Halloween, but not so in this house. In the Bean household, we celebrate Oktoberfest, a family holiday second only to Christmas in our children's eyes.

Almost ten years ago, as a young married couple with two small children, Dan and I thought we'd plan a fall-themed party as an alternative to Halloween and the trick-or-treating that neither of us were particularly fond of. We decided to call our party an Oktoberfest and invited all of our extended family for a day of pumpkin carving, hay rides, and a bonfire.

"That was nice," Dan and I concluded at the end of the day. "Let's do it again next year."

Little did we know that we had witnessed the birth of a new family tradition. We have hosted an annual Oktoberfest ever since. With each passing year, our family and the families of our guests have grown. Last year's Oktoberfest featured nineteen adults socializing and playing horseshoes and seventeen children carving pumpkins, eating candy corn, racing through a scavenger hunt, and toasting marshmallows around a giant bonfire at the end of the day.

Although many aspects of Oktoberfest vary year by year, some elements remain constant. For example, Dan always writes a poem for the Oktoberfest invitation. The first year, he wrote, "The corn's in the bin for another year, so come to the Beans and have some beer!"

Also immutable are the grilled sausages, hot apple cider, goodie bags for kids, and raffle prizes for grown-ups. Kids' activities range from egg and spoon races to scavenger hunts. One year, Dan and I spent weeks beforehand pouring concrete into molds to make a realistic looking, life-size dinosaur skeleton. We buried the "bones" in a sandy spot and then set an enthusias-

tic group of junior archeologists to work excavating the site and re-constructing a prehistoric "fossil."

Last year, because of a variety of extenuating circumstances, it seemed that none of our extended family members would be able to come to the Oktoberfest. Although we flirted with the idea of canceling it, the children were adamant that the party must take place. When we decided to hold Oktoberfest after all, the first line of the invitation read, "You thought it wouldn't happen; you tried to stay away. You knew you couldn't do it; it's time to come and play."

And come they did. It seems that our nieces and nephews have come to anticipate Oktoberfest as much as our own children do. At their insistence, their parents rearranged their schedules, made the long drive to our house, and the party was on.

The original Oktoberfest was a royal Bavarian wedding celebration in 1810. King Ludwig I commemorated his marriage to Maria Teresa of Saxonia by declaring a state fair in Munich. The festival was dedicated to the fall harvest, and tradesmen from all over Germany came to view the crops, sing songs, dance, and sample the first beer of the season.

We haven't a drop of German blood in us, but there is no denying that Oktoberfest is an important tradition and a valuable part of our family life. Our celebrations of Christmas and Easter are often so filled with outside obligations that it can be difficult for extended family to gather and really visit with one another. At Oktoberfest, though, cousins, aunts, uncles, and grandparents gather in a special way. The sole purpose of this event is to draw together family members for a fun and relaxed day of visiting.

We are surrounded by a vibrant, loving network of extended family, and their support is a precious gift from God. In particular, I treasure the fact that our children know and love their cousins. At Oktoberfest, as they run races, eat goodies, and carve pumpkins, these young cousins create special memories and form priceless bonds of friendship. Long after the Jack-o'-Lantern candles are snuffed, the last of the pumpkin bread is eaten, and the gooey marshmallows are wiped from children's faces, we will appreciate the gift of our family and strong connections will endure.

28

Fowl Trouble

Teaching Respect for God's Creation
2004

$\mathcal{A}$ couple of years ago we decided that it would be a good experience for the children to raise a flock of laying hens. In the early summer, we ordered a dozen baby chicks. We told the kids they could each choose one chicken that they would be allowed to keep as their own. We promised that regardless of their egg production, these personal "pet" chickens would never wind up on the dinner table.

Eamon, then six years old, chose the smallest of the group, a pint-sized chick with bright eyes and smooth, clean black and white feathers. Because she was a Barred Rock chicken, he at first intended to name her "Rocky." When we told him she was a female, however, he decided that "Rockette" would be more appropriate.

Rockette had an easy life. Long summer days provided plentiful green grass and an assortment of delectable insects. She basked in sunny spaces in the chickens' outdoor pen during the day and roosted in the

161

comfort of a sheltered coop at night. It wasn't until the colder days of late fall and early winter that we discovered she had a problem.

As it turns out, "pecking order" is a very real thing for chickens. In every flock there exists a firmly established and viciously reinforced status among all hens and roosters. Rockette, with her small stature and docile temperament, ranked lowest among her peers, and they were determined not to let her forget it.

They pecked at her constantly. They kept her from the food and water until she became so hungry and dehydrated that it became necessary for the children to feed her by hand and bring her a separate dish of water. We nursed her wounds and helped her find secluded places in the coop where she could hide from the other chickens and their merciless bullying, but it wasn't enough.

One morning that winter, as the temperatures dipped near zero, I made the short walk out to the chicken coop to let them into their yard and feed them. When I opened the coop door, the chickens hurried out as usual and pecked eagerly at the corn I scattered on the snow. Rockette, however, lagged feebly behind, limping on bloodied feet. From the doorway, she peered at me fearfully. She hesitated for a moment and then sat down, flopped her wings out carelessly, and closed her eyes.

If you've ever tried to pick up a healthy chicken, you'll know why I worried when I picked up

Rockette. She did not peck or scratch or try to wrestle away from me. She collapsed in my hands and her legs dangled helplessly beneath her. I hurried her to the house, but I had no idea what I would do with her when I got there.

By the time Dan arrived home from work that evening, Rockette was well established in a metal cage on top of newspapers in our bedroom. I was relieved when my explanation of our feathered guest was met with only a raised eyebrow and a suggestion that I call the vet.

"How can I say this?" the woman on the phone told me. "Most vets don't treat chickens because we consider them, well...expendable."

Of course it was true. Most farmers would solve this particular problem by preparing Rockette for the soup pot.

Thankfully, Dan is not like most farmers. He prepared Eamon for the fact that his pet might die, but agreed that we should do our best to take care of her. With much coaxing, Rockette sampled a bit of grain and sipped a few drops of water that night. In the days that followed, while her coop-mates froze in sub-zero temperatures, she enjoyed a heated home and feasted on bits of blueberry muffins that the kids smuggled away from the breakfast table. For his part, Dan pretended not to notice the distinct smell of "chicken" which permeated our bedroom no matter how frequently I changed the newspapers.

Then one day, when I returned from an afternoon of running errands, I found Dan putting the finishing touches on a small wooden house, complete with a tar-paper roof and tiny hinged door.

"Whaddya' think?" he smiled at me.

"Oh, Mama," Kateri rushed to me breathlessly. "Isn't it pretty? It's Rockette's new house!"

And so it was. Dan set the house on concrete blocks, fastened some chicken wire outside the coop so that she would have an outdoor yard, and our recovering friend moved in.

The kids willingly took on the extra chore of caring for Rockette separately from the other chickens. For weeks, Dan and Kateri trekked out to Rockette's "house" twice a day to rinse her sore feet with hydrogen peroxide and monitor her progress. When warmer weather arrived, they brought her juicy June bugs, fresh grasshoppers, and the choicest green maple leaves the woods had to offer. The children particularly seemed to relish their "chicken nurse" responsibilities.

Their patient thrived. Though permanently scarred and mangled, her bloody, wounded feet healed completely. Thick, shiny feathers replaced her sparse stubby patches. By the end of the summer, we all had to admit that Rockette looked downright plump, and we certainly knew she was spoiled.

Whenever she heard the front door to the house open, she would do a little dance, hopping up and down and flapping her wings, demanding a treat. She expected fine service and usually she received it.

In the fall, we gave away some of our older hens and replaced them with new, young layers. Since the new chickens would disrupt the established pecking order within the flock, we decided that this would be a good time to introduce Rockette back into the group before winter.

Cautiously, the children and I brought her to the pen where the other chickens were wandering about and set her on the ground. She and the others eyed each other suspiciously. One of the new hens, a large, plump, golden-feathered beauty, approached our little friend and engaged her in a staring contest. We held our breath.

Suddenly, the children gasped as the new chicken dove at Rockette and pecked her on the back. To our amazement, however, Rockette stood her ground. She scarcely flinched at the initial assault and then held the other hen steadfastly in her stare. After a long pause, she sprung at her attacker and sent her squawking into the coop. The children cheered.

As we watched, Rockette made her way through the yard meeting all chicken challenges with authority and defiance. In a short time, the other hens accepted her dominance. Even the rooster learned to stay out of her way.

So a queen was born, and as it turns out, she is a benevolent ruler. Though the other chickens scurry out of the way when she approaches, she is never unnecessarily harsh with her subjects. In the coop today, her scarred feet are the only remaining evidence of our previously violent flock.

Today when I see Her Majesty strut through the yard pecking casually at the grain I toss to the ground, I am grateful that we didn't take the easy way out. The effort and patience of my husband and children in caring for a helpless injured chicken demonstrate the importance of respecting God's creation. This experience has taught my children the value of caring for all forms of life, however weak and vulnerable. Rockette is a living reminder of the Scripture truth that "...many who are first will be last, and the last will be first" (Mt 19:30).

As I watch our little queen this morning, she pauses in her pecking and cocks her head in my direction. For a moment she holds me in her gaze with one blinking eye. Her glossy feathers gleam in the sunlight, her tail feathers ruffle in the gentle breeze, and Rockette returns to her foraging with contentment.

29

Picture Perfect

Making Christmas Memories
2003

Perhaps it was my pregnant hormones. Whatever the reason, at the start of the Advent season last year, as I lay on the couch in a nauseated haze of morning sickness, I hatched a wild plan. This was the year, I told myself, that I would get the children's Christmas picture done early.

Usually, I wait until the last possible moment to have their picture taken. It's tradition. Throughout December, as I collect photographs of other people's charming families, my anxiety builds. Other people's children seem perfectly poised. They model reindeer sweaters and sport flawless haircuts. They sit in neat rows, smiling radiantly. My children, it seems, are never all clean and dressed and smiling (I'd settle for just not crying!) at the same time.

Last year, however, I decided that I would manage to get all my children to strike a perfect pose at precisely the same moment in front of a professional photographer. Not only that, but I determined to do it weeks before Christmas. I made an appointment for my five little angels and triumphantly marked the date on the calendar.

I should have known better.

On the afternoon before the day of our appointment, as I was tidying up the bathroom, I made an alarming discovery. A pair of kitchen scissors lay on the counter surrounded by dark clumps of hair.

Based on the color of the hair and my children's ages, I made a quick guess. "Ambrose Augustine!"

Dutifully, four-year-old Ambrose appeared in the doorway. His large green eyes blinked at me innocently. Random patches of baldness mottled his handsome head.

Even with a close crew cut, it took a couple of weeks before Ambrose's homestyle haircut was smoothed out enough for a Christmas picture.

The night before our new appointment, I was awakened by three-year-old Juliette at my bedside.

"I don't feel good," she whimpered.

I raced her to the bathroom. Even as I stood holding my vomiting daughter over the toilet, I thought, "This cannot be a stomach virus."

My hopes of a passing case of indigestion were dashed before morning when two of my other children got up and made it to the bathroom just in time.

On the phone the next day, I begged and bargained my way into an all too familiar last-minute appointment less than a week before Christmas.

When the day arrived, I bathed, dressed, and groomed the children. I duped my husband into accompanying us, and together we drove to the studio. We lined up the children in front of a female photographer who looked altogether too young and inexperienced to pull off the miracle I had in mind.

To encourage smiles, my heroic husband stood behind the camera waving his arms wildly and pretending to fall down. His audience hooted with laughter. Instead of "cheese," he instructed the kids to shout pint-sized obscenities like "poopy diaper." They screeched with pleasure.

"Take the picture!" I urged the hesitant photographer as baby Stephen tired of his father's foolishness and reached for me. "It's not going to get any better!"

Afterward, using a process of elimination, we chose a sort of halfway-decent, off-center, not-as-bad-as-the-others picture and ordered an overpriced package of wallet-sized copies. We received the prints just in time to stuff them into Christmas cards and rush them into the mail. So much for perfection.

On Christmas Eve, we put the kids to bed early and stayed up sipping egg nog and wrapping last minute gifts until 11:00 when we woke them.

We coaxed them into red velvet dresses, buckle shoes, and dress pants. We brushed their hair, bundled them into winter coats, and carried them, yawning, through the cold black night to their carseats.

"Jesus is born!" we whispered as we entered the church.

And he was. Our Lord was present in the manger, on the altar, and in our hearts.

Slumped in fuzzy pajamas, Stephen dozed on my shoulder. Pungent incense filled our nostrils and the smoke climbed slowly toward heaven. Joyous carols announced our Savior's birth as I watched candlelight flicker in my children's eyes. I closed my eyes to fix the moment in my memory.

Here at last was my perfect Christmas picture.

30

A Joyful Noise

The Boisterous Sounds of Family Life
2004

Years ago, my eight brothers and sisters and I were shocked and offended one evening when we discovered our father wearing earplugs at the dinner table. Poor Dad. He didn't mean to offend us. He is practical man and in his mind the earplugs were merely solving a noise-level problem.

But we were offended.

"How insulting!" I remember thinking. "Doesn't he want to hear his own children's precious voices?"

All these years later, though, my own children's precious voices are helping me to see his point of view.

Take now for example. Kateri and Eamon are practicing their spelling words above the sound of Ambrose belting out a rendition of the Marine Hymn. Stephen makes rumbling engine noises as he propels toy cars across the wooden floor and crashes them into the furniture. Juliette is squealing and chasing the baby as she scoots across the room in her walker, shaking a rattle and gurgling, "Ma-ma-ma-ma..."

The atmosphere is raucous, but the worst part is this: no one is being naughty. There's no child to grab by the ear and demand that he stop. Boisterousness is part of a child's job description, right in there along-side the "messiness required" clause. Multiply one nat-urally noisy kid by six, add in a few squabbles, a ring-ing telephone, and an electronic toy or two, and you've got an official ruckus.

The most embarrassing part is that I hardly notice the "regular" noise around here anymore. I once called a friend during what I thought was a relatively peace-ful moment. When I identified myself she laughed and said, "Of course it's you—I knew who it was as soon as I heard the noise!" Marvelous.

Noise is not essentially a bad thing, though. We read in the Psalms: "Make a joyful noise to the LORD, all the earth; break forth into joyous song and sing praises" (98:4).

We are called to be a joyful people, and for fami-lies with children unruliness is inevitable. Our chil-dren's unrestrained voices are evidence of the inner happiness and untainted joy with which God has filled their little hearts. This doesn't mean, of course, that the clamor doesn't sometimes wear on one's nerves. Occasional peace and stillness can be a welcome relief.

This winter I was blessed with a head cold. For several days afterward fluid remained in my ears and mercifully dulled my hearing. I never slept so soundly.

I was so serene in the midst of our family's typical late-afternoon chaos that I'm sure the children didn't recognize me.

Today, however, my hearing is as keen as ever. By dinnertime this evening my nerves are so frazzled that I fear the next joyful shout or bag of marbles dropped on the stairs might send me over the edge. It's times like these that I am most grateful that we raise chickens. Feeding them and putting them in their coop for the night gives me an excuse to escape the commotion and steal a moment of quiet.

Before anyone can protest my departure, I grab my coat, slip on my boots, and scurry out. The door slams behind me and I take a deep breath of brisk winter air. At last, the wonderful, refreshing sound of silence!

Darkness falls around me as I make the short walk to the chicken coop. The only sounds I hear are the gentle rustle of wind in the nearby woods and the quiet slurp of mud beneath my boots.

Once at the coop, I toss some grain in the henhouse and stand for a moment watching the chickens peck the ground, clucking contentedly. I relish the peaceful stillness of the evening air. I close the door, latch it for the night, and then turn to face home.

The soft glow of electric light glimmers from the windows of our house into the surrounding darkness. I hear the muffled sound of shouts and laughter from within. The sound of my children's voices carries across the field, through the clear, cold night air, and falls gently upon my ears. From this distance the sound seems to beckon to me now, calling me home.

Danielle Bean graduated *summa cum laude* from Saint Anselm College in Manchester, New Hampshire. Her highest credentials, however, are being earned as she lives out her vocation to marriage and motherhood. A freelance writer, she is a frequent contributor to the *National Catholic Register* and *Faith & Family* magazine. Her husband Dan, a Catholic school teacher, built their home in Center Harbor, New Hampshire, where they homeschool their six children. www.daniellebean.com/sys/main

BOOKS & MEDIA

The Daughters of St. Paul operate book and media centers at the following addresses. Visit, call or write the one nearest you today, or find us on the World Wide Web, www.pauline.org

CALIFORNIA

3908 Sepulveda Blvd, Culver City, CA 90230   310-397-8676
2640 Broadway Street, Redwood City, CA 94063   650-369-4230
5945 Balboa Avenue, San Diego, CA 92111   858-565-9181

FLORIDA

145 S.W. 107th Avenue, Miami, FL 33174   305-559-6715

HAWAII

1143 Bishop Street, Honolulu, HI 96813   808-521-2731
Neighbor Islands call: 866-521-2731

ILLINOIS

172 North Michigan Avenue, Chicago, IL 60601   312-346-4228

LOUISIANA

4403 Veterans Memorial Blvd, Metairie, LA 70006   504-887-7631

MASSACHUSETTS

885 Providence Hwy, Dedham, MA 02026   781-326-5385

MISSOURI

9804 Watson Road, St. Louis, MO 63126   314-965-3512

NEW JERSEY

561 U.S. Route 1, Wick Plaza, Edison, NJ 08817   732-572-1200

NEW YORK

150 East 52nd Street, New York, NY 10022   212-754-1110

PENNSYLVANIA

9171-A Roosevelt Blvd, Philadelphia, PA 19114   215-676-9494

SOUTH CAROLINA

243 King Street, Charleston, SC 29401   843-577-0175

TENNESSEE

4811 Poplar Avenue, Memphis, TN 38117   901-761-2987

TEXAS

114 Main Plaza, San Antonio, TX 78205   210-224-8101

VIRGINIA

1025 King Street, Alexandria, VA 22314   703-549-3806

CANADA

3022 Dufferin Street, Toronto, ON M6B 3T5   416-781-9131

¡También somos su fuente para libros, videos y música en español!